Following graduation from USAF Bombardier School, David Irvin was assigned to the 447th Bomb Group of the 8th Air Force. In November of 1943, his B-17 was shot down and he was captured by the Germans. Undaunted, Irvin escaped and traveled through Belgium and Denmark and was returned to his unit courtesy of a State Department aircraft flying out of Sweden. He completed 30 combat missions and then returned to the US to complete his pilot training.

In 1948, Irvin volunteered for the Berlin Airlift and flew 85 missions from Rhein-Main AB at Frankfurt, Germany. He later volunteered in the B-47 program and completed training in navigation, radar, and bombardier school (again) to become what is respectively known as a "4-headed monster" in the Air Force. Assigned to the 9th Bomb Wing, he pulled temporary duty in Guam and flew missions over North Korea.

Other assignments include duty with the 44th Bomb Wing and 2nd AF HG in Louisiana. In 1964, Irvin was transferred to Strategic Air Command HQ where he served for four years on detached service, and he flight tested the Lockheed U-2R in Vietnam. He was then transferred to the 14th Strategic Aerospace Division at Beale AFB in California where he was the SR71 project officer and division special project officer.

Other books by Colonel Irvin include Reconnaissance is Black, Escape or Evade, and Special Operations; all of which are available through Turner Publishing Company.

T0163587

HIGHWAY TO FREEDOM
THE BERLIN AIRLIFT

COL. DAVID W. IRVIN, JR.

TURNER PUBLISHING COMPANY

Turner Publishing Company

Copyright ©2002 COLONEL DAVID W. IRVIN, JR..
This book or any part thereof may not be reproduced
without the written consent of the author.

ISBN: 978-1-68162-314-6

Library of Congress Control Number: 2002104682

Turner Publishing Company Staff:
Publishing Consultant: Virginia-Sue Forstot
Designer: Tyranny J. Bean

Limited Edition.

TABLE OF CONTENTS

The author, undergoing C-54 flight training at Great Falls, Montana. December 27, 1948.

Chapter One
BACKGROUND

As a result of backroom discussions in 1948 with the British and the French, the American military was asked how they would supply the already-beleaguered Berliners with food, heat and other supplies. The military turned to the military air transport service and asked them the same question. There were several limitations put upon the MATS staff, such as providing the American troops with support, but on a more limited basis. Considering the fact that the C54 would carry more for greater distances, the planners combined the use of the C47 and the C54 resources to start airlift from bases in West Germany. Selected were Frankfurt-am-Main and Wiesbaden. The reasons for this was that both airports could handle increased activity, and the physical space could be enlarged to support more aircraft, and staff, and the petrol and oil needed to provide what was needed to do the aggressive pressure from the pentagon and state department, the staff planners devised a plan that would provide that was needed to sustain the life of those civilians literally held hostage by the Russians. First, the Eastern U.S. and Western Europe were robbed of C47s, and stationed the people and aircraft at Rhein-Main Air Base, in Frankfurt, W. Germany, and, at the same time, started a transportation pipeline for coal from the Ruhr Valley, food from the German farmers, and foodstuffs from Canada and the U.S. The Berlin airlift started during the first week in July 1948 only after advising the Russians of what we were going to do.

The international flight authority had established a ten-mile wide corridor from Fulda, West Germany, in the American zone, on a direct line to Berlin. This was done, theoretically, to allow civilian airliners to maintain transportation to and from Berlin. The corridor was an international agreement by all parties of the Potsdam Accord, and Roosevelt had signed the document. While the C47s were flying into and out of Berlin, on an irregular basis, the 60th Troop Carrier Group was transferred from Hawaii to Rhein-Main, and the 61st Troop Carrier Group was transferred from their home in Alaska, to be re-stationed at Weisbaden, West Germany. Both units consisted of three squadrons plus maintenance personnel and equipment, and sixty C54s. Thus, the supplying units now consisted of 120 aircraft, and partial flight crews, and a total maintenance contingent.

The mass movement of 120 aircraft and supporting equipment and people was not an easy task. It took the better part of three months to get the two groups in place, provide housing for them, and feed them. The maintenance support was going to be tough, for MATS recommended each flight crew to fly two flights per day for six days, and then give them a rest. Before the arrival of the C54 Skymaster, the C47s were flying two missions per day, and the flight crews were getting worn out. They could not be immediately replaced, so MATS formulated, with the help of the Training Command, an Airlift (called Project: Vittles) training course, and picked Great Falls, Montana, a World War II base.

In 1946 the United States was still figuring out what to do with the huge military force needed to sustain the war effort, just concluded, successfully. The Russians, on a fourth of the war-end partners in deciding what to do with the defeated-Germany, decided they did not get sufficient quantities of land to satisfy their needs. Contrary to the agreements made after the Germans had signed the peace accord, the Soviet government made a bold decision and announced on June 24, 1948 to isolate Berlin. The partition separated the German capital into four segments, one partition to each of the conquering nations, i.e., the United States, Great Britain, France, and the Soviet Union. The USSR effectively closed off the surface and waterways into and out of the already-beleaguered metropolis of Berlin. This was not expected by the other three countries. It caught them completely by surprise. Each of the countries was undergoing the demobilization process, each in their own way, and now needed to do something drastic to stop the Soviets' aggressive unprovoked action.

Because of their mighty air force contingent, our countries decided to utilize the expertise of the Military Airlift Transport Service (MATS) rushed C54s from around the world to Germany. The Douglas-built four-engine transport was the largest aircraft to carry the foodstuffs needed to sustain a city of 2,000,000 people for an indefinite period of time. This was a bold decision, one that would cause a huge logistic problem to begin with, and the number of flight crews and maintenance people would be staggering. The British and French air forces were dwarfed by the American industrial force, but everyone had to pull their weight, whatever the cost.

First, the French had a token transport force, but provided an input; the British had a significant force of small transport aircraft, and were to contribute significantly during the 18 months of supplying the German beleaguered civilians in Berlin. The Russians believed the Americans still had a sizable force of transport aircraft, and the new C54 four engine transport was coming off the production in record numbers. They were replacing the backbone of the air transport fleet of C47 twin-engine aircraft that spearheaded the island hopping in the Pacific, and the invasion of Europe under the domination of the German Nazis. The C54 was larger, carried more weight/people over longer distances. The C47 was an aircraft not forgotten, was not capable to a sustaining life-supporting venture that was to be envisioned by the American military staff after they were told by the politicians to feed, house and protect the Berliners. The only way to do this was by air, a subject not covered by the Potsdam agreement.

Great Falls, Montana was lacking a mission, being primarily an Air Defense Base but was too large for fighter aircraft. The planners set up an accelerated training program for new C54 pilots, and even laid out a standard route much the same as the one they would fly to and from Berlin. The training program simulated the actual flight path that was flown on Vittles. As the C54s became more prevalent, from the factory and the operational units, it became obvious the pilots new to the program were not used to flying four engine transports. This problem was compounded by the fact the training unit, in Great Falls, was not manned by airlift experience. Mostly, the instructors were experienced MATS pilots who had flown the C54 but none of them had been on the Airlift. MATS did get a few C47 pilots who had flown more than 100 missions on Vittles, and they were a great help, but needed experience.

In flying an operation that is foreign until the pilot is exposed to it on a continuing basis, day in and day out, the whole operation is very complex. But to create a whole task force, from scratch, is almost beyond belief. But that is exactly what happened during the 1948-49 Berlin Airlift and is almost beyond comprehension. As the reader will see, it actually happened. I am particularly fortunate to become a part of this venture.

Chapter Two
EXPERIENCE LEVEL

The year 1948 was the start of it all, in my young career, in the United States Air Force. I was an instructor pilot in the North American-built B25, the aircraft that bombed Tokyo in April 1942. My station was Keesler Air Force base, in Biloxi, Mississippi, an air training command base. The flying was good. I wanted to get more experience. I was commissioned a second lieutenant Bombardier, at Deming Army Air base, in northern New Mexico, transitioned in the Boeing B-17, and flew 30 missions over France/Germany from January 1943 to July 1944. Having been shot down in late 1943, I was captured by the Germans, and escaped, making my way through France, Belgium, Holland and Denmark, to return to my bomber unit and complete my tour of duty.

When I returned to the United States, I immediately volunteered to become a pilot. I was accepted and graduated as a pilot in June 1945. Most of my flights were for administration, courier and people from one base to another. Perhaps the most interesting of all of the flights were the flights on October 17, 1947 and January 19, 1948. In the lifetime of a pilot's career there are flights that stand out in the flier's mind.

On October 18, 1947, a hurricane was fast approaching Florida, and we were called to provide nine pilots to evacuate North American AT-6s, a single engine twin seat trainer. I have flown this aircraft many times and, on occasion, ferried one from one base to another. Also, I had flown one many times when I was at the Air Tactical School, at Tyndall Field, Panama City, Florida, so I was selected to be one of the pilots to evacuate.

With a 650 horsepower radial engine, the AT6 was a nice little aircraft to fly, but it definitely was not one to fly in weather. A C46 twin-engine cargo/personnel aircraft picked us up at base operations at Keesler, and delivered us to Boca Raton, Florida. There were many low clouds, and it was very bumpy, but we had no problem in landing. The AT6s were lined up in front of Operations, so we inspected them, and filed a flight plan to Panama City, for fuel, and then flew on to Keesler. This evacuation was routine, but interesting, in that there were nine planes to move, and we flew in loose formation all the way.

The most interesting out-of-the-ordinary things were the way we got into formation, and we had to wear seat parachute packs, because in the B25 we wore backpacks. To get into formation, the first four AT6s took off, and the leader made a slow turn to the left. He circled the field until the next three closed into formation. Then the next five took off, and chased the leader as he came over the field. I was number seven, and had trouble getting with the others. The last two had trouble catching up, especially when the leader announced, on the radio he was turning on course, but would maintain his low airspeed until the last two were with him. This consideration was because we had to land at Keesler before the sun was down. Flying at night with the AT6 in formation was not something to be anticipated.

We landed at Tyndall Air Force Base, having flown from Boca Raton to Orlando, to Tallahassee, to Tyndall. We landed at 1:30 p.m. and requested immediate refueling, time being of the essence. Once completed, we again took off single file, and, after one wide turn, were en route to Pensacola, Florida, to Mobile, Alabama until we finally landed at Keesler at 5:30 p.m., just as the sun was setting. Good flights, but I was exhausted, and slept for almost 24 hours.

On January 19, 1948, I was scheduled to fly from Keesler to Boca Raton Air Base, Florida, to drop off students for the mechanics school, and pickup the morning report (shows who is there, who is left, and who is coming into the school), so the report would arrive back at Keesler by 10:00 a.m., and it was correlated with other morning reports, and forwarded to Air Training Command by noon time. Therefore, we had to takeoff by 4:00 a.m., an ungodly hour for most of us. We were the first flight into Boca Raton since the hurricane had passed by. The base was in a shambles, what with palm trees uprooted, buildings losing their roofs, and the power was out. We were given a hand-held radio to get in contact with the base tower.

Fortunately, the weather was crystal clear, and, as we approached the base, we could see the devastation. We contacted the tower, and the communication was poor, at best. We were cleared to land on runway 12 (southeast), and over flew the approach to see that the runway was clear. It was, and we prepared for landing. On the final approach, about 500 feet, there was a garbled transmission, followed by a red flare being shot from the tower indicating we could not land. We increased power, raised the landing gear and flaps, and adjusted our flight path so we could see the runway, and there was a large alligator crossing the runway. Obviously, he had the right of way, and I certainly was not arguing with him. We made another approach, and, by this time, the reptile had cleared the runway, and we got a green flare, cleared to land.

The trip back was uneventful, but my copilot and I laughed all the way, and felt properly belittled. It was a good story, one that I will never forget.

The officers from Great Falls, assigned to the 330th Troop Carrier Squadron, at Rhein-Main Air Base, in West Germany. Picture taken in the barracks in Northern Frankfurt. February 1949. Back row (L-R): Amsberry, Byrd, and Bird. Front row (L-R): Parker, Author, and Land

Chapter Three

PREPARATION

There was a call for pilots to participate in Operation "Vittles" that required pilots with at least one thousand pilot hours, being unmarried, with two engine experience. In October 1948 I decided to apply, and see what would happen. ATC approved my application and I got my orders to report to the 1701st Replacement Training Unit (RTU) at Great Falls Air Base, Montana, to report on or before December 17, 1948. I requested that the Operations squadron fly me to Great Falls on December 16, and they heartily agreed. I asked Personnel to give me five days of leave, which was approved. My orders gave me the leave, and authorized me to fly to Great Falls, so I was all set. I have often said that whatever job you have, learn the system, and then make it work for you, and this has proved a good way to go.

I spent the four days in New Orleans, and had a great time. It was tough to leave, but the memories would linger. The flight on the December 16 was uneventful, but seemed long especially when you're not flying the aircraft yourself. The weather was in our favor, and I got a good look at the base, and especially the flight line ramp. It seemed to be loaded with C54s (the Skymaster) I was going to fly.

I thanked the B25 crew, and got a ride to the headquarters squadron, signed in, and was given a barracks number, that, fortunately, was only about a block from the headquarters. There was a jeep available to get me to my new "home," and I had a footlocker to get to my quarters, plus a suitcase that was heavy by itself. The quarters were a long tarpaper affair, with doors at both ends, and two coal-burning stoves that proved to be warming. We were in the northwest, and it starts getting really cold in November, so the old timers told me.

Besides an instruction sheet, there was a bulletin board at the far end of the barracks. It showed where the mess hall was, the classrooms, the officers club, and the Base Exchange. In as much as it was still early (4:00 p.m.), I decided to walk around, and get myself acquainted with where I had to go. First was the mess hall—I love to eat. That was only a short walk from our quarters. The officers club was two blocks away, the base exchange was a short walk and the class-rooms were in a group one block from the place where we stayed. All in all, the area was well-placed, and the time involved getting where we were supposed to be at any given time didn't seem to be a problem. The only problem seemed to be the temperature.

I stopped in at the mess hall, that was open and serving, and I had a large helping of meatloaf, a baked potato, hot beets, vanilla tapioca pudding, and coffee. It was to my liking. returned to the barracks, and found four more pilots stowing their gear. I introduced myself, and found the bunch was all stationed on the west coast. Two were from March Field, outside Riverside, California; one was from Travis Field, outside Sacramento, California; and one was from McChord Field, near Tacoma, Washington.

The one pilot from Travis was a C-47 pilot, but he was not familiar with four-engine performance. His name was Billy Payne. The one from McChord was a former fighter pilot, but had C119 experience. They were Jerry Williams and Harry Jenkins. They were going to have dinner, and wanted me to come with them, and, of course, I never refuse to go somewhere to eat. Two cups of coffee later, we returned to the quarters and decided to call it a day, in anticipation of the ground school we would be exposed to the next day. It was getting cold, so we stoked the fire and went to bed.

We were scheduled to start school at 7:00 a.m., so we got up at 5:30 a.m., showered and shaved, and went to the mess hall for breakfast. During the night, seven more trainees showed up, and I didn't get a chance to introduce myself. I decided to take that up at the lunch break, or maybe at the end of the day.

The first class of the day was by a captain intelligence officer and it included where we could expect to be stationed, what the route into Berlin was, and some of the obstacles we would encounter on our flights into and out of the West German capital. There was a lot to absorb, but we got a handout, and that helped. We were encouraged to study the items to give us an edge on what to expect.

The second hour was devoted to the weather and the radar approaches we were to be given. That was very interesting, and I learned a lot. The third hour was given by the group maintenance officer. He had been chief of maintenance for the 60th Troop Carrier Group, then in Hawaii, and now at Frankfurt. He knew his business, and I wondered why he was not in the business in Germany. Almost sensing my question, Major Loeffler explained that his experience was needed at Great Falls, but he was trying to get back to his unit in Frankfurt.

The C54 was not a very complex aircraft, and the ground school went by without much of a problem. We got a copy of the Douglas checklist, and the major went over the items, in detail. We were not expected to make a detailed ground check, but were going to have to know what we were doing. MATS believes the ground crew should do what they were being paid for, and the pilots were expected to fly the aircraft.

We spent one entire day going over emergency procedures, with a pilot who said he had over 200 hours in the C-54. The checklist was mostly mental, and we had to repeat each procedure until the instructor felt we knew what to do, and when to do it. Part of the last day of ground school was spent with a cockpit mockup, with another instructor explaining the function of each of the different switches and panels, and briefly talked about the circuit breaker panels.

The last half of the final day of the ground school, after lunch, was spent on the flight line, with an instructor going over the preflight techniques, and then all twenty-one of us crammed ourselves into the cockpit (most of us could only hear what was being said). Each of us got our "turn" to sit in the left and right pilots' seats, and the instructor patiently went over the internal preflight, start engines, and radio procedures. When it was my turn, I tried to memorize the various controls, and was vague as to the sequence of certain functions. Then I got out of the cockpit, and wandered around the flight engineers position and the two bunks that were built into the side compartment. The main part of the plane was separated by a door. The cargo compartment was really large (in comparison to what I had been used to flying). At the end of the cargo area was another door to an area that included a toilet and washing sink, plus some standard equipment, such as rope, tie down strips and emergency radios. Most of the flights had been over water, but were kept in readiness for the airlift. I never understood the reason for carrying some of the equipment on every flight.

At the end of a long day, we were taken to the squadron briefing room, on the flight line, and it was explained we were to be there at 8:00 a.m. the next day. We were told there would be a bus to pick us up at the mess hall.

On the morning of December 27, 1948, after a bumpy bus ride to squadron operations, we filed into the briefing room, and noticed on the flight board (chalk board that had the day's flights posted, by aircraft number, IP, students, takeoff time, and estimated flight time): Lt. Rahl, Instructor pilot Lt. Lane, C54D #44-9041, flight time 4 hours. We took our seats, and the briefing officer, a captain, called out our names, and told us to stand up, then called Lt. Lane, who was a short, stocky pilot. He was in front of the seating. He turned and motioned us to follow him out of the briefing room. There were series of tables, with chairs against the back wall. Lane picked one, and shook each of our hands, and motioned us to sit down. He started out, "This is your first flight. It is a demonstration flight. You will occupy the right seat, and read the checklist, when I call for it. The checklist is in each aircraft, and will be used for start engines, taxi, takeoff, climb cruise, letdown, before landing and landing, post-landing, and engine shutdown. All you have to do this first flight is read, and watch what I am doing. You will each fly for about 30 minutes. Rahl will go first, and Irvin will be second. Each of you will make two landings from the right seat."

We walked out to the airplane (third one from the flight line road). The crew chief was waiting, saluted, and told us the aircraft was ready for flight. Very formal.

Chapter Four

TRAINING FLIGHTS

Taxiing the C54 was a simple matter. There was a round handle on the left of the pilot, about six inches in diameter, that controlled the front nose gear, so steering was not a function of power and brakes. This made sense, so there was no pressure on the braking system or the engines.

The radio communications, start-up, taxi and pre-takeoff was standard. The takeoff was just like the B25 (both were tricycle gear) and the nose had to be raised about 10 degrees to get the airplane in-flight. After takeoff, a climb to 6,000 (our assigned altitude) was normal. After level off, by Lane, he reduced power, and trimmed the aircraft for level flight. It must be remembered the C54 was empty (of cargo) and as light as a feather to control.

Rahl was not used to such a big aircraft. He had flown the C46 (a standard twin engine, twin gear bird), and Lane reminded him this was an easy plane to fly, but its characteristics were different from most planes. He then told Rahl to take the yoke, and fly the airplane straight and level for a while. Rahl had trouble, because he manhandled the C54, and thus over controlled. Lane then reduced power, and told Rahl to adjust the trim, to compensate for the change in power. After about thirty minutes of wrestling the airplane, the IP told me to change seats with Rahl. It was tough, but we only had a short time. We were in an accelerated program, as we were told time and again. Another kind of pressure, but I could understand the problems of MATS in getting the number of pilots to take the pressure off the crews in West Germany.

After adjusting the seat (I'm 6 foot 3 inches, and had to readjust the seat for my long legs), I noticed we were flying at 5,500 feet, with an airspeed of 130 mph. I took control of the aircraft and retrimmed, asking Lane if we should be at 6,000 feet, and 150 mph, and he nodded, saying nothing. I added power, raised the nose, and let the aircraft settle down on the speed and altitude. I then asked Lane what heading to fly. He motioned straight ahead. I nodded, and retrimmed the aircraft, and lightly flew the C54. It was very light to the touch, and easy to fly. I knew I wasn't going to have trouble with this one. Lane told me to do a reverse (180 degrees) turn, at a 30-degree angle of turn. I gingerly turned the aircraft to the left, easing into a 30-degree turn, retrimming and increasing the power a little bit. I rolled out on the new heading (back to Great Falls), retrimmed, and reduced the power to maintain 150 mph.

As we approached the field, Lane instructed me to descend at 500 feet per minute, and level off at 2,000 feet. He called the tower, and requested permission to enter the traffic pattern, and that was approved. I retarded the throttles, lowered the nose, and asked for the before landing checklist. Lane looked at me and asked if I had flown the C54 before. I said no, and settled down to a 500 feet per minute descent, and adjusted the power to maintain 150 mph. He was putting the pressure on me, for he knew I had never flown this aircraft before.

At this point I didn't care, just focusing on my control. I told the IP to call on downwind, and request permission to land, fully expecting him to take over control, and let me handle the radios. He surprised me by telling me to go ahead and land the bird. I called for gear down, lower half flaps, and call on base leg. He smiled, and did what I asked him to do. It suddenly came to me that I was going to make the landing, and I'm not sure I believed him, but continued on the base leg. I had purposely flown the downwind leg farther from the runway, to give myself plenty of room, if the IP was going to wait until the last minute to take over flying.

The tower cleared us to land, and I turned on the final approach, retarded the throttles, requested full flaps, when the airspeed slowed to 120 mph I used a bit of throttles, and aimed at a point that looked to be short of the runway. I knew that would allow for the aircraft to float, and I never was going to land "long." An old pilot once told me that the altitude above me and the runway behind me did absolutely nothing for me, and thus I always aimed short. As we crossed the end of the runway, I retarded the throttles to idle, and brought up the nose until what I thought was going to be a landing altitude.

For my first landing in the C54, I didn't think it was too bad. I gently lowered the nose, applied brakes, and suggested Lane take the aircraft, for steering could only be accomplished from the left seat. He took control, and turned off the runway onto the taxiway.

Then he stopped the plane, looked at me, and said he didn't believe that was my first landing. I countered him by asking for the after-landing checklist. He smiled, pushed the RPMs to the maximum, raised the flaps, and adjusted to trim. He started taxiing again.

When we reached the final taxiway leading to the runway, Lane unstrapped, and told me to change seats with him, and make the takeoff and one more landing. I almost didn't release my straps, but finally remembered, and got into the pilots seat, and asked for the before-takeoff checklist. In as much as I hadn't used the nose-wheel steering, I hesitated in using the right amount of turn, but got myself under control. Lane got clearance to takeoff, and he motioned me to get on the runway. I did so, and the takeoff traffic pattern and landing went without much of a hitch. Lane said to stop the aircraft on the taxiway, and change seats with the other student. He said I was through for the day. By the time I got out of my seat, and sat down in the flight engineers seat, my flying suit was soaked. I didn't realize I had sweat that much.

The rest of the flight went about the same as when the other student had started with. He had trouble with controlling the altitude of the C54. The instructor wasn't very good. He really didn't know how to instruct, but that was not my problem. After Rahl had made two low approaches, the number three engine quit. No fire, no smoke, it just stopped running, so Lane took control of the bird, and made a close in pattern, and mentally went through the check-list, and shut down the engine. He retrimmed the aircraft for a three-engine landing, and flew the pattern at the same speed as if we were flying with all four engines running. His landing was not exceptional. He finally asked the tower to clear him (we were on the final approach) before he told the tower we had "lost" an engine. The tower asked if we were declaring an emergency, and he said "no" and started his final approach. The tower had alerted the crash trucks (as they should have done) but the time was so short, the red trucks could not get into position until after we had touched down, and were taxiing back. I kept my mouth shut, but really wondered who this guy was. He certainly was not what a student should be exposed to.

We got a short debriefing. Our flight time for this mission was 4 hours and 15 minutes. Our next flight was scheduled for December

29, with the same instructor and student. This time I was to fly first, and that helped me, so I could experience in starting engines and getting prepared for the flight. Everything went fine, as did the next flight, on December 31. We were told to expect the flight time to increase to five hours (instead of four hours), and could expect to fly a simulated Airlift profile. Things were getting very interesting.

Late the evening of December 30, we were briefed on what to expect when we flew what they called "Little Vittles," and it seemed like a simple mission. I was to find out differently. On January 1, 1949, in C54D 44-9076, and Rahl was held back to the next class, hoping he would become proficient. The other student was a Captain Don James, who was scheduled to fly with Lane and me. He was to fly first, then I would fly the second round of "Little Vittles," that was fine, for I could observe how the route was to be flown.

We took off at 10:00 a.m., to the southwest, and made a climbing turn to the right, flying to the west of Great Falls, so we could make a right turn, at 6,000 feet, on a southwest heading and 25 minutes to Helena, then a left turn to go over Helena and get ourselves on a direct course to Havre. This leg was a critical one, for it simulated us leaving the American Zone, into the Russian Zone, and used a course-line instrument that the pilot could set. Our heading was to be 35 degrees (northeast) and we had to get the cursor in the dead center of the instrument to compensate for any windage. We were told to remember that the corridor was only ten miles wide, and the Russians could take measures if we strayed out of our zone. The electronic instrument was installed at Helena as it was in Fulda, West Germany, on the very edge of the two zones. On the Airlift the course instrument was able to transmit for about 90 miles, and then was unreliable. By that time, however, we should have the correct course set up, and had to maintain that exact course until we reached the controller in Berlin.

The flight time from Helena to Havre was 50 minutes. When we got to Havre we were to turn left to a heading of southeast to Great Falls. It must be remembered that we were unable to use our radio compass on the leg from Helena to Havre, for we did not have a compass capability in the Russian Zone. After Havre, we climbed to 7,000 feet in our turn back to Great Falls. That last leg was 42 minutes long. Once we got back to Great Falls, the instructor would take over flying the aircraft from the right seat, and the students would exchange positions. Now it was going to be my turn.

Lane had descended to 6,000 feet, and reset the airspeed at approximately 150 knots. This would be the altitude and airspeed we would have to fly in the airlift, going to Berlin. We would have to keep track of the time on each leg. The time to Helena was 26 minutes, and we went over the city in 25 minutes, then made a slow turn to the left to line ourselves up on the critical leg from Helena to Havre. I checked the course line indicator, to make sure the correct heading (035 degrees) was in place. When I crossed Helena I had to make a small correction to the left, and got the cursor in to center, indicating I was directly on course. I adjusted the trim to hold 6,000 feet. We literally were on our way and the weather was clear and in the early afternoon the sun was to the left, and finally got the heading where I wanted it. It was 033 degrees (no wind heading was supposed to be 035 degrees). I had to hold that heading until the ground station faded, and still maintain the heading until the time ran out. We were supposed to be over Havre in 50 minutes. Actually, we were right on course, and our time was 49 minutes. We started a climbing turn to 215 degrees and leveled off at 7,000 feet. I was satisfied, and Lt. Lane didn't say anything so I assumed it was a good mission.

Lane took control and lowered to 2,000 feet, getting clearance from the tower, was cleared into the traffic pattern. He told me to make a low approach, and that we would change seats (with the other student), and he would make the landing. The other student, who was supposed to be a MATS pilot, made a sloppy landing, bouncing pretty hard, but the plane stayed in one piece. The flight was over, and our flight time was five hours. We were scheduled to fly in two days. I went home and slept like a log. I didn't miss a meal, and even got a chance to visit the Base Exchange, to pick up a few articles I needed.

Much has been said and documented about the use of radar, especially the use of Ground Control Approach, commonly called GCA, but, it must be remembered the use of ground controlling of aircraft for minimum weather landing was not introduced to the military fliers until the end of 1947. This was a fortunate circumstance because of the blockade of Berlin by the Communists. The timing could not have been better, for Europe had some nasty weather during their winter months, and when the Berlin Airlift started, one of the first units to be set up was the radar control unit at Templehof Airdrome, in the American sector of the German capital.

For an obvious reason, one of the early GCA units was set up at Great Falls, for support of the Operations Vittles, and the crews who were trained were the pilots, who, for the main part, had not used this type of low approach and landing technique. Having completed seven flights at Great Falls, I was exposed to GCA on my eighth, ninth, and tenth flights. The main thing to remember, and this was vital, was that the pilot had to believe the ground controller, and aggressively follow his instructions. This could mean a life or death situation. If this sounds dramatic, understand that every landing at Templehof was a ground-controlled approach, regardless of the weather. The reason was simple, to get and keep the pilot proficient in the use of radar landings and the radar operators sharp in what they did. As the reader will find out, we were separated by three minutes in our takeoffs, flight, and landing in Berlin. This was simple, for it was determined that the GCA operator could handle one aircraft every three minutes, and no less.

My first ever GCA was on my eighth flight, and we had been briefed on what to do, and the instructor stressed the importance of following the instructions of the ground operator without thinking of what was happening. I really did not know what to expect, but the calm monotone voice of the controller belied his capability to bring the aircraft within the sight of the runway, as if every approach was done with a minimum ceiling due to weather, such as fog, rain, or even extreme haze. Each student got one GCA approach on his first exposure to GCA, and this was because we had nine aircraft in the air at the same time, and positioning was critical to enable each aircraft to be funneled into the radar approach control, and passed each one on to the GCA unit at the appropriate time. Approach control radar would position each aircraft on a long final approach, at 2,000 feet, and then hand you off to the GCA final controller, the most experienced of all of the radar operators. In the beginning, the radar operators were just as inexperienced as the fledging pilots, but good coordination and faith in the system made it work. Each approach caused the operator and pilot to gain more and more faith in what needed to be done. By 1948 the ground team made the airlift work, and work well.

The accelerated flying/ground school program was good, except the level of instruction left something to be desired. The eight flight, on January 25, was my first exposure to the radar approach concept, and didn't bother me very much. Following instructions was made easy by the ground controllers. My ninth flight was on January 27, and it was the first time I flew the "Little Vittles" course, including the letdown and GCA approach. I was told by the instructor my next flight was to be my check ride, and he felt I would have no problems, unless I forgot what I had learned.

Flight No. 10 was on January 29, 1948, in C54D 44-9025, and took three hours to complete. I was satisfied with the courseline stabilization, and the GCA was very good. The landing was really good, and the check pilot, Captain Ahern, said I had passed and would be on my way to Germany in the next week. I suddenly felt very tired, but happy. Glad to get this training out of the way. Now there was nothing to do but wait, and I spent the time sleeping, eating, and walking around the base. I was very highly motivated, but my patience was not the greatest. I believed the pressure had not been alleviated with my check ride, and I realized I was still pressured, in my own mind. Time should ease the tension, so I tried to relax. Of the 21 who started in my class, there were 18 left, and most of them needed 14 flights, so my 10 flights made me feel good, and I felt I was prepared for the Airlift.

BERLIN AIRLIFT ~ 1948 - 49

Chapter Five

THE BERLIN AIRLIFT
THE PRELUDE

H aving to check in with operations every day was a pain. Finally, a notice was placed on the bulletin board that we were to leave on February 1, to land at Westover Air Base, Chicopee Falls, Massachusetts, when we would be transported to Frankfurt/Rhein-Main AB, W. Germany, and get our permanent assignment (to airlift squadrons). The 18 of us got on the bus with all our gear, and were driven right to the aircraft. The flight engineer took control of our possessions, and instructed us to get on board. There were enough seats for all of us. The seats were like the commercial airline seats. He told us the flight would take six hours, so to relax and enjoy the flight. Six hours and 15 minutes later we landed at Westover, told to get on the waiting bus, and would be taken to our quarters.

We pulled up in front of a two-story barracks. The charge of quarters (CQ) told us to bring our gear inside, and take any bunk. The building was empty. He told us the mess hall was open, right across the street. He also told us the base theater was down the street one block across the street, and the movie was listed on the bulletin board. Someone asked him if he knew when we would be leaving, and he said he would try to find out for us.

I hauled my footlocker into the building, and grabbed a bunk near the entrance door. I sat down, and contemplated what was going on. Jim Byrd told me to get myself going, so I grabbed a towel from my flight bag, and cleaned myself up. We then trooped across the street to the mess hall. We had salad, greasy pork chops, mashed potatoes, and green beans, with peach pie—delicious! I had a second piece. Three of us decided to go to the movie, where, to my surprise, the main feature was *Casablanca*, with Humphrey Bogart and Ingrid Bergman. That movie was and is my all time favorite. So we hurried down the block, in time to see the news, and settled down to see the movie.

When we got back from the movie, I was humming *As Time Goes By*. That is my all-time favorite song, and Dooley Wilson did a great job. The CQ was waiting for us, and told us we should be ready to get on the bus at 9:00 a.m. the next day, because we were scheduled to fly to Frankfurt, in a C121, Constellation. It was a MATS transport plane, with more than 80 seats just like a commercial aircraft.

I took a long, hot shower, shaved, and went to bed. I was beginning to relax, and I was anticipating the long (eight hours) flight to Germany. The next morning, I awakened at 7:00, got myself put together and went across the street for breakfast. Three eggs later, with sausages, toast, orange juice and three cups of coffee, I was ready. At 9:00 a.m. the bus pulled up. We loaded our gear and were driven to the flight line, pulling up next to the Constellation. We got into the plane, and were told to sit in the back seats, that the front end was reserved for VIPs (Very Important Personages). This was strange, for the VIPs were already in their seats. It turned out they were the West German finance minister, and his staff. Wonder what they were doing in our country? I found out later the West Germans were supported legally and financially by the United States.

We were given cold sandwiches and plenty of coffee. I took a long nap, but the eight hours began to drag because I was beginning to wonder what we would be doing when we got to Rhein-Main. I watched four of our troops play bridge. The politicians were grouped together in the front of the plane, so we couldn't get to the cockpit. The time really dragged for the last two hours, and then the pilot notified us that we were approaching Frankfurt. There were broken clouds at lower levels, and the ground temperature was 58 degrees. The time, considering the change of time zones, was 3:00 p.m.

The landing was uneventful, and we taxied up to the commercial airport. We noticed the area on both sides of the runway was wingtip to wingtip with C54s and C47s. The flight attendant told us to stay in our seats, to allow the West Germans to deplane. I remember feeling as if we were back to second-class citizen status, again, but that is another story.

As we got off the airplane, I noticed the flight engineer was unloading our gear from the cargo hold in the rear of the fuselage, and, with his assistant, loading it in the waiting truck. A first lieutenant introduced himself as Lt. Charlie Gaston, our escort officer until we got situated. He informed us that the base was loaded, and there was no billets for us, so we had to travel through Frankfurt to the north section, called the Atterbury-Betts area, that was to be our permanent home. With that, he closed the bus doors, sat in the first seat, and instructed the civilian driver, in German, to move out. The driver seemed to know what to do, so we just sat back, and, to our amazement, it took 45 minutes to get to where we were to live. The scenery was inspiring, but still had remnants of our World War II bombing.

In the middle of the town of Frankfurt, the trolley cars were running, and there were workers everywhere. We followed the trolley tracks out of the downtown, and headed north. There was still a lot of rubble, but the shops were open, and the town had the looks of a prospering city. Amazing. I had bombed Frankfurt twice when flying B17s of the Eighth Air Force in 1944.

As we drove further north, paralleling the trolley tracks, I noticed a large two-story building, stark white, with a well-groomed lawn and foliage. I asked the lieutenant what it was, in as much as it seemed untouched by bombs. He said it was the I.G. Farbin Company. As my memory recalls, I.G. Farbin was one of the leading German manufacturing companies that made a lot of war materials. We finally reached a large complex, with a German guard at an open gate. The lieutenant said, "Welcome to your new home." The bus pulled up at the second of many two-story buildings. As we exited the bus, we noticed an airman on the steps, with a clipboard. As we got to the steps, he asked us our names, and each one was told his room number. We were all billeted on the first floor. I was assigned to Room 118. Dragging my footlocker up the steps, I wrestled with the bulky locker, carrying my suitcase. At this time, no one offered to help. The escort officer went with the CQ, and left us to find our way. My room was halfway down a long tiled corridor. It was about seven feet wide and 20 feet long. It had a camp bed, a dresser, a closet, and a desk. The floor was tile, also. The room had two windows, that opened outwards. It was neat as a pin. The date was February 3, 1949.

We decided to all go to dinner (it was 5:00 p.m.), and so we collected all of the troops and had dinner. It consisted of corned beef, cabbage, boiled potatoes, and/or brussel sprouts. I was to find out later that the staple of the Germans was potatoes, cabbage and brussel sprouts. We had hot fresh bread, fresh butter, jello and coffee. I knew that most of the food produced a lot of gas, but that didn't bother me one bit. I am an eater, and everything tasted so good. The fresh bread was, for me, the crowning glory of any meal. (My maternal grandmother was German, and she and her husband owned and operated a bakery in San Francisco.) I am basically a tall, lean person, and knew I was going to gain a lot of weight in the environment, but my stomach won over my brain.

When we got back to the barracks, I got ready for a nice, hot shower. All of a sudden, a loudspeaker (called Tannoy) blared and told everyone in the building that the newly arrived pilots were to catch the bus promptly at 0800 (8:00 a.m.). I hadn't realized each room had a direct line with the CQ's office. We could be called individually or as a group. We got so used to listening, we got spoiled. I took my shower, shaved, turned in, and had a good night's sleep.

The next morning, the same escort met us at the bus, and, after we got on, he announced we were going to the 513th Troop Carrier Group Headquarters, and we would be given a long briefing by the staff. He told us that the 513th was relatively new, being called to active duty two months ago. The home group was the 60th Troup Carrier Group. He told us the 513th consisted of the 330th Troop Carrier Squadron, plus the 331st and the 332nd. All three squadron headquarters were in separate buildings next to our mess hall, which made sense, because all of the 513th crews were living in the Atterbury-Betts area. It was February 4, 1949.

As we passed through downtown Frankfurt, we saw it as a bustling thriving city, with very little to show it had been razed by the Allies just three years ago. When we got to the gates of Rhein-Main Air Base, it took on the look of another city. We wound around, and finally stopped in front of a two-story World War II building, looking as if it had just gotten a new paint job. There were no guards at the front door, so we just followed the escort officer, and he took us to a large auditorium where we were told to sit down. The front of the auditorium had a raised podium, with a huge map of Germany, with the routes of the airlift, both in and out. Colonel Hadley, the group commander of the 513th, welcomed us and said the operations staff would give us a detailed briefing. Thank God we were going to get some detailed information, at last!

The director of operations, a major, took over the briefing, and gave us a myriad of information. He said we would each get a handout, and to ask questions of his part of the briefing. He started out by welcoming us to the Combined Airlift Task Force, with the parent unit being the Supreme Headquarters Allied Expeditionary Force (SHAEF) and advised us to pick up some SHAEF patches on the way out. He said CALTF was made up of units from the United States, Great Britain, and France. Our command included the 513th, the 60th (Frankfurt), VR6 and VR8 (Navy-Frankfurt), and the 61st (Wiesbaden) as well as Fassberg and Celle. He told us we would get the Army of Occupation Ribbon, with the Airlift Device (a miniature aircraft) after we had been 30 days in country. We were to complete processing at our squadron headquarters. The 18 of us were split up, with six going to each of the squadrons in the 513th. He told us they were short on copilots, and would probably fly our first 30 missions as copilot, and then be upgraded, if we showed we could do the job as pilot.

We were briefed on the routes over Russian territory, and he stressed time and again, that we had to stay in the corridor, and expect Russian MIG fighters to harass us. That would not be the end of it if we strayed out of the corridor. If this happened, the Russians would file a formal protest. That was not our problem he said, but the squadron commander would issue the crew with a stern warning not to do it again.

The operations briefing took a long time, and covered subjects such as radio compass frequencies, that takeoff times would be assigned by the control tower. We had a special frequency all our own, so as to not impede the international air traffic. We would fly two missions a day for six days, and then have one day off. The CQ would post the weekly schedule on our bulletin board, and reminded us the mini-bus was to take us to our squadron operations at the rate of one per hour, so we had to gauge when we got on the bus. We would come back on the same bus schedule. This schedule was ongoing for 24 hours per day, seven days per week.

Our first flights were tentatively scheduled for March 1, but the accurate schedule would be on the bulletin board at least three days in advance. He briefed us on alternates to be used, fuel loads which were based on predicted weather, so we could get back to Frankfurt and go to an alternate if the occasion warranted. Orly Airport, France, was to be used as our primary alternate. The weather people would brief us on our other alternates.

We had to remember this outfit had been in business since July 1948 (not the 513th; we got good planners transferred from the other units, so we had to rely on their learned expertise). The supply briefer, a captain, told us we would be carrying about 20,000 pounds of coal, milk, pipe, cement or flour, with sometimes a special load, but didn't elaborate. The weather officer, a captain, gave us a really comprehensive briefing on the seasonal weather forecast, stressing that we would receive to-the-minute weather they received from the inbound/outbound airlift flights. That part didn't bother me, for I knew the weather would only be a problem if GCA didn't do their job.

I talked to a lot of pilots who had been flying the airlift for several months, and they all stressed the need to follow the radar instructions to the letter, and we would not have a problem. The public affairs officer, a first lieutenant, briefed us on the customs, the things we could look for, and the fact that our housing area had a pretty good exchange, and we would get the essentials there. Also, there was a photo lab, because taking pictures seemed to be a fetish with the airlift pilots. I was to learn, first-hand, how true that was going to be.

After the last briefing, the operations officer asked if there were any questions. One of the new pilots asked him what would happen if the courseline radio was not working and what should we do. The briefer said the answer was in three parts. One, if that happened during the day and the weather was good, we could continue on, by pilotage, but that was not encouraged. Two, if the weather was not good during the daytime, don't try to fly the corridor; return to Rhein-Main with our full loads. Three, never try to fly the corridor at night without the courseline indicator being operative. That made sense, and we all were glad to get precise procedure. We were getting the idea that it was not safe to fly the airlift when the Russians could be provoked. We found out, on my first mission, the Russians had no less than five airbases along our route, and apparently just itching to harass us. Nice thought.

The briefings lasted until 11:00 a.m., and our brains were a jumble of information. I picked up two SHAEF patches, went outside and saw our bus waiting for us. The escort officer was there and knew we were mentally exhausted. When we all got in the bus, he said we should go to lunch, and then report of our squadron headquarters for processing. Then he added, with a smile, we were free to do what we wanted, and said the trolley schedule times were on the bulletin board. He suggested we not spend any time that would get us into an overnight situation. That sounded ominous, but we let it slide.

As we drove off the base, and into Frankfurt, I had an opportunity to study our escort. He was talking with one of the other pilots, so I could observe him. He had a freshly pressed Army uniform, a SHAEF patch on his shoulder, a World War II service ribbon, and an Army of Occupation ribbon. He seemed like a nice young man, but I was disturbed by the fact that he was a first lieutenant. If he had been in the service before the war's end, that put him in the service in 1945, and after only three years was a first lieutenant. I was made the same rank in 1944, and I guessed either I wasn't that sharp, or he was a barnburner, as the fast-risers were called.

Berlin, from the air. Notice the Friedrichstrasse Railroad complex in the center. The World War II bombing devastation is evident. March 1949.

Chapter Six
AIRLIFT BEGINNING

The next three weeks dragged by but Byrad and I decided to go into Frankfurt (safety in numbers. . .a new place, a new language, always the unknown) so we walked down to the trolley line and waited. There were several men and women wandering about. The trolley was about half full, and we got aboard. The conductor, dressed in a very spiffy dark blue uniform, smiled at us. I motioned about how much the trolley ride was going to cost, and stumbled through my spotty German. He nodded and indicated five with his fingers. I assumed he meant five pfennigs (about ten cents). We gave him the proper money and sat down. At one of our briefings, someone explained the conversion factor (between dollars and pfennigs/marks) and we changed our American money for the Deutsch marks. It was relatively easy converting, because two pfennigs equaled ten cents. Anyway, it was close enough so we could make our way through the purchasing agenda, whatever that was.

We departed the trolley in what we assumed was the downtown area. There were a lot of people, including quite a few Americans, in uniform. We had been briefed that we were to wear our uniforms, and no civilian clothes. That made sense, because we were the Army of Occupation. Don't know why they even had to say it. We wandered around for a couple of hours, sightseeing, and then got back to the trolley stop. We caught the trolley and went back to the housing area about 5:00 p.m. Just in time for dinner.

Dinner was good. Corned beef hash, baked potatoes, broccoli, hot bread (always), chocolate cake with frosting, and coffee. I knew I liked the food, and hoped I wouldn't gain too much weight.

The next day, we caught a mini-bus that took us to the 513th area, wandered around the flight line, and then into the flight operations building. It was plainly marked, and we just went in, and looked at the briefing room, with a large blackboard with the flight schedule, takeoff times, aircraft number, call signs, and a short weather synopsis, including what the weather was forecasted in Paris, our first alternate.

Finally, on February 27 the CQ posted the March 1949 flights, and we all crowded around. Byrd was to fly with Carter on March 1 and I was scheduled with March 2 and March 3 with Captain Herman Duty. Our proposed takeoff was 0900 (9:00 a.m.) on the 2nd and 3rd. Well, it finally was going to come true, after such a long time. I decided to catch the 0600 bus, so I would have plenty of time to get prepared on the flight line. We were told to wear our flight suits, leather jackets, and flying boots.

I had purchased a black baseball cap, with CALTF sewn into the front, because we were told wearing one would help protect us from the sun, and thunderstorms. It cost me one hundred pfennigs or $0.50. I don't remember much after the first two airlift flights. They go so fast. In our beginning we were flying six days straight, and had one day off. April through May 1948, we began to get more crews from the States, and the CALTF operations started five days of flying and two days off. It must be remembered that meant we got some time off, but were still flying two missions per day.

The first flight was with Captain Duty, in C54 #44-5582, called Sign Big Easy 82, into Berlin, and Big Willy 82 coming back to Rhein-Main. Big Easy meant we were loaded, and going into Berlin, and Big Willie meant we were devoid of cargo, and on our way back. Relatively simple. Duty met me at operations, introduced himself, said he had 73 missions under his belt, and not to worry, just watch him. I was to make the radio calls, and he would tell me what to say, and when to say it. I thought that was good, for we didn't have very many radio calls to make. I was to fly the right seat going in, and he would put me in the left (pilot's) seat and fly the aircraft coming back to our base. That really got me excited, and he saw by the look on my face I was ready to go. I had no trepidations. He patted me on the back, and we headed back, to our aircraft at 8:40 a.m. He told me he would do the walk around, and told me to call the tower to confirm our takeoff time as 0900.

I was reassured with his giving me some responsibilities. I got in the airplane. There was a metal stairway to the back of the fuselage, and I scampered in, making my way past the huge load of coal, into the cockpit. The flight engineer gave me a half-hearted salute, and made way for me to get into the right (copilot's) seat. He introduced himself and said he had flown with Captain Duty and that I was in good hands. I assumed he knew this was my first airlift flight, but how he knew I didn't ask. I turned on the power and the radio with the tower frequency already available.

"Rhein-Main tower, this is Big Easy 82, over."

"Big Easy 82, this is Rhein-Main tower. You are confirmed with a 0900 takeoff. Use runway 33. Copy?"

"Roger, tower. Copy. Will call when taxiing. Out."

As I finished my radio contact with the tower, Duty came into the cockpit area, with a smile on his face. He said he was very happy I did such a good job, that he hated to have to contact anyone. He said that I would do, and climbed into the seat, buckled up. Then he called for the checklist. When I got to the "start engines" part, he said for me to start numbers three and four (the two right-side engines). It was not very difficult, but a set procedure would make it a lot easier. When I had finished and the propellers were running, on the right side, Duty started the left engines and told me to tell the tower we were taxiing for runway 33. I did so, and we moved out of the revetment, onto the taxiway. There was another C54 getting ready for a takeoff, and Duty said we would be in good shape for our three-minute separation.

As we approached the runup area, the aircraft (Big Easy 79) was halfway down the runway, and that seemed to be good, for us.

"Rhein-Main Tower, Big Easy 82, number one. Will takeoff 0900."

"Roger 82, cleared onto runway, cleared for takeoff. Altimeter 29.87. Call when starting turn." Duty gave me a "thumbs up," advanced the throttles, and swung onto the runway. We put the throttles into maximum power, released the brakes exactly at 0900, and started to roll. Duty got the nosewheel off the ground, and we were airborne.

"Gear up."

"Gear coming up. Standing by the flaps."

"Roger, flaps up. Starting turn to the left. Check Darmstadt on the compass."

"Roger, starting turn, Darmstadt on the radio. Heading to Darmstadt shows 170 degrees."

"Rhein-Main Tower, Big Easy 82 starting left turn. Darmstadt at 21." That indicated we estimated the Darmstadt beacon at 0921. I looked over at Duty, and he told me we didn't have to tell the tower our time over the first checkpoint. Then he said they probably knew our time better than we did, and it would be best not to clutter up the radio. He told me to turn the radio frequency to the Vittles frequency. I did, and heard the aircraft ahead of us call over Darmstadt at 18, our timing looked good. Each aircraft had to call in over each checkpoint, in the blind, and there was no reply required from anyone. Each aircraft had to keep track of the aircraft ahead of it, to space ourselves three minutes behind them. It was all by rote, and there was to be no problem if each aircraft did what he was supposed to do.

Duty rolled out on a heading of 168, and flew directly toward the first checkpoint, following the radio compass. We leveled off at 6,000 feet. Duty lit a cigarette, and I reached for a cup of coffee. He pointed to the yoke (control column) and said to fly the bird. I complied. When the radio compass swung around to the tail, that indicated we had passed over the station. He said to call out we were over Darmstadt at 21 (right on time schedule). I did so, and turned left to a heading of 070 (generally to the east) changed the radio frequency to the Aschaffenburg beacon, that showed three degrees to the left. I corrected, and took a swig of my coffee. Duty had a smile on his face, and told me I was staying with the aircraft, and sure made his job a lot easier. I nodded, and concentrated on flying the aircraft. The next checkpoint was scheduled to be 0937.

A few minutes later I faintly heard Big Easy 66 called in over Aschaffenburg at 0930, that meant two aircraft ahead of us was one minute early. I looked at Duty and he said not to worry. Our main concern was to be sure we were three minutes behind Big Easy 79, the aircraft ahead of us.

The weather was perfect. There were a few high clouds, and for this time of year, the weather fronts seemed to be absent. That was a blessing for us, for we had heard the ground fog following a front brought the weather down to close to the ground. Actually, I was looking forward to flying an actual GCA approach under adverse weather conditions. I thought of it as a challenge and I never told anyone my philosophy, for fear they would have me committed. Weird joke.

"Big Easy 85, Darmstadt at 25." I nearly jumped out of my seat. I wasn't prepared for hearing the C54 behind us, but calmed down. He was one minute late, but had plenty of time to increase his speed, and make up his time. Duty read my thoughts, and commented 85 wouldn't have any problems.

"Happens all the time."

Very prophetic, I thought.

The countryside was mountainous beneath us. Very green, and the roads were in stark relief to the tree side. The radio compass swung back around. The time was 0937. Right on schedule, I thought, as I put down the time on my knee pad. I corrected my heading left to 015 degrees (almost due north) and tuned the radio compass to the Fulda beacon.

"Big Easy 82, Aschaffenburg at 37." I made the radio call, and Duty said he would fly this leg of 37 minutes, to Fulda. He said he wanted me to get the procedure for aligning ourselves with the course line instrument, and that this part of the inbound flight was the most critical. It didn't take that much skill, I thought, but the practice we had at Great Falls was not under the most critical condition like this one was. We'd see.

As I have said, the Douglas C54 was the right aircraft for the job of transporting foodstuffs to Berlin. It trimmed out very precisely. I think the only problem was in getting all four engines at the same pitch (RPM). That was solved by an instrument, mounted in the center upper part of the cockpit instrument panel. There were three small propellers. All four engines were tuned to the number one engine. We had to change the pitch of any or three engines so that the propellers would stop rotating. Then we could assume the engines were in synchronization. Simple, but effective.

Duty pointed out the landmarks along the route from Fulda to Berlin, especially the Russian airfields. I could see the Soviets had loaded these airfields, so in case we strayed, they were in position to harass us.

I had procured a map, primarily of the Russian Zone, and carefully annotated the airfields. After a number of flights, if the weather was good, I could identify them, and even saw the MiGs taking off, but, generally they did not barrel through our flight path, unless they decided they needed practice. With C54s every three minutes in a confined corridor, they didn't have to do much navigation to find us.

Our estimated time of arrival (ETA) at Templehof was 11:18 a.m. Duty told me to contact Templehof approach control, and advise them of our time of arrival.

"Templehof Approach, Big Easy 82, ETA 11:18."

"Easy 82, we have you on radar. Maintain present heading. Confirm altitude 6,000."

"Roger, Air controller, Altitude 6,000. Standing by."

At 11:16, Templehof told us to turn right to heading of 051. This was to allow us to get a good long approach to the field, even though the weather was perfect. I could see the aerodrome from across the cockpit, but Duty reiterated we had to fly a GCA on every flight into Berlin.

"Big Easy 82, turn left to 350."

"Roger, Templehof, Easy 82, left to 350."

We flew this new heading for about three minutes, and then, "Big Easy 82, Tempelhof, turn left to 270. This is your final approach. Put gear down, flaps as desired. Copy?"

I wondered, and looked over at Duty, and he indicated to put the gear down, and half flaps. I complied. GCA called, saying "82, this is your final controller. Confirm gear down, turn left to 267 degrees. No further discussion. We will take over from now on. If you cannot complete the approach, climb to 7,000 feet, on a heading of 270, and contact departure control for further instruction." I "rogered" him, and put my hands lightly on the controls. Duty looked over at me, and feeling my hands on the yoke, smiled and nodded his head.

"Big Easy 82, this is your final approach controller. Start your descent now, at 500 feet per minute. You are on glide path. Your heading is good. Continue your approach. At 200 feet take over and complete your landing run. Your heading is good, you are 10 feet high on the glide path, lower the nose. You are now on glide path, turn left two degrees. Good corrections. You are passing through 1,000 feet, one half mile, on glide, on course. Everything looking good. You are now one-quarter mile, passing through 500. If you have the runway in sight, continue your approach for landing. Over and out."

Duty told me to give him full flaps, that he had the runway in sight (at that time we were coming in over a five story apartment house, with the 6,000 foot runway about 100 yards from the houses. It looked tough, but once you get the idea you have to reduce powers before the apartment, and lower the nose, so you will be able to round out, and the airspeed will not cause you to float down the runway. In the back of your mind you had to remember the aircraft had 20,000 pounds of weight, and that would not allow you too much floating, if you controlled the airspeed.

Duty came over the obstacle about 10 mph low, on purpose, lowered the nose, and rounded out right over the end of the runway, landing about 1,000 feet from the approach end. He lowered the nose, and started braking. The aircraft shuddered at first, but Duty kept the brake pressure going, and the bird slowed down to taxi speed at least 1,500 feet from the end. He looked at me, and said, "That, friend, is the way its done. Any questions?"

"Open the cowl flaps, RPM to maximum, aircraft seems okay," Duty said, glancing at the flight engineer. We followed the yellow jeep and lined up behind the airplane in front of us, with the beautifully curved overhanging the operations. It was a beautifully architecturally designed effort. There is a picture enclosed, and that is something to see. If the weather was rainy, we would taxi under the overhang. It was that big. During the war, the Nazi-fighters would be parked, making it easy for them to get the pilot, unscathed, into the cockpit, and out to the runway, so they were dry and not wet. It was a reassuring sight. I never failed to be impressed with the operations building, that had temporary quarters, a restaurant, and operations area. It was a complete building for the flight crews, if needed.

As he set the parking brakes, Duty said, "Now we can have some fun. Let's get out and stretch," with a big smile on his face. We got out of the pilot's door (not the fuselage double doors. We didn't want to interfere with the unloading process). The flight engineer, knowing what was expected, lowered a rope ladder, and Duty went down. I followed him. There, in front of us, was a Red Cross truck. As we approached, I could see two nice-looking young ladies, with coffee and donuts. Duty looked at me, winked and offered me first place. I never refuse a change in line for food, so I grabbed three donuts and a nice hot cup of coffee. No charge.

The ladies were good looking, their hair nicely combed, and their ample lipstick accentuated their smiling faces. It was a real treat, and Duty clapped me on the back, and said this was what got him charged up for the trip back. Then he laughed. We went under the wing and talked about my training at Great Falls.

Chapter Seven
TEMPLEHOF AIR BASE

D uty was assigned to the 60TCG when the Russians closed the door, and he was flying the C47, and immediately asked to be assigned to the C54. He flew as a copilot for five flights, and then was given his first pilot's status, so he knew what the story was. He was particularly interested in the quality of the instructors. I tried to downplay the quality of those instructors but I don't think I was very convincing. He said he had the chance to go to Grand Forks, but turned it down, because he liked flying the Airlift. After one half of one flight I couldn't blame him. I was so enthused it showed. He said it was time for us to get back into the cockpit, the West Germans had off-loaded their 20,000 pounds of coal in about 15 minutes.

There were five cargo carriers, who dropped each sack of coal on a metal chute, then five loaders would pile up the coal on a large flatbed truck. They were experienced, and didn't waste any motion. I didn't watch them at first, but got the opportunity to observe on future flights. Lastly, two haulers swept the floor of the bird, and you had better not be standing downwind of the coal dust, or you would look like a miner.

As Duty climbed aboard, I looked at the wheels getting aboard. I went and looked at the wheels to see if there was any wear. I met the flight engineer at the ladder, and said they were okay, but if I wanted to keep myself apprised of what was going on, he had no objection. He asked me if I were a MATS pilot. When I said "no," he smiled, and said the MATS pilots left all of the ground pre-flight/post flight to the flight engineer. It was refreshing to see a pilot, new or old, keep the plane in mind. I said nothing. What could I say? When I got into the cockpit, Duty was seated in the right seat, and I got into the pilot's seat. This was almost beyond my understanding, but I didn't say anything. Duty told me to watch the plane ahead of me. When he started his engines, we would start ours three minutes later. That made sense.

After we started engines, and were ready to taxi, Duty told me to take over control on the steering. I nodded, released the brakes, advanced the throttle, started moving, and I followed the yellow stripe down the center of the taxiway. Duty called the tower, and we were given the okay to taxi to runway 15, altimeter setting was 29.92. I nodded, and changed our altimeter to the correct setting. Most of the time it was the same for the whole flight, either in or out of Templehof.

As we rounded toward the runway, the C54 ahead of us started his roll and as we approached the takeoff spot, Duty reminded me that we were 20,000 pounds lighter, and the bird was easier to control, that the tendency of the newer pilots was to over control. I nodded.

The tower cleared us for takeoff, and I taxied into position, checked the flaps, and advanced the throttles, without setting the brakes. The aircraft started accelerating immediately, and we reached takeoff speed almost before I was able to get the nose-wheel off the ground. I didn't look at Duty, but he must have been smiling. I called for raising the gear, which he did, and changed radio channels, and asked Departure Control for approval to turn on course. (That was kind of ironic, for we had to turn only 15 degrees to get on the way to our next checkpoint.) Duty had tuned into the Templehof radio beacon, and I corrected to the right, and was almost on course from the start. Departure Control cleared us on course.

We leveled off, and I continued to track outbound, trying to set my course that would keep us in the outbound corridor. We had taken off from Berlin at 1200, and estimated Hannover at 1255, and Rhein-Main at 1:50 p.m. The first time we were in the corridor, so we had to watch where we were going, but had little problem because the wind was directly on our nose.

The countryside was a lot sparser than the trip in, but was still very pretty. I noticed the smoke from the Hannover factories at quite a distance. At 7,000 feet we could see a lot. I tuned the Hannover beacon about 70 minutes out, and we were right on course. We passed over Hannover, and Duty called and told the aircraft behind us our time was 12:50. I turned the aircraft to the left, to a heading of 195, and tracked outbound for the first 30 minutes, then tuned in the Frankfurt beacon. I had to correct five degrees to the right, but could see Frankfurt in the distance. When we got closer, Duty asked Rhein-Main approach control for permission to descend, and was told to continue at 7,000 for five minutes. There was other traffic.

After we landed, and taxied back to our squadron parking area, we went back into the squadron operations to look at the flight schedule board, and found we were scheduled to fly our second mission at 1500. We had landed at 1350, so we had a little time. I found out when we were flying two-a-day, the second flight was in another aircraft, for the loaders at Rhein-Main could have the first aircraft loaded, because the amount of coal to be provided (from the Ruhr Valley) was a rough business because we had an average of ten flights in our group per day, and the two Navy squadrons had six aircraft to load. It was physically impossible to service that many aircraft.

Going back to Operations, I went to the bathroom, washed my face, and just sat down for a few minutes. Duty sat down beside me, and asked if I was all right. I smiled, and told him I was all tense, but would be okay for number two. He almost laughed, and said this was his last flight. He had completed 100 flights, and had his orders to fly out of Lisbon, Portugal, in C54 courier. Each country has a large transport that is for the government's embassy personnel, plus classified documents. That sounded like "a real cushy job," and I said so. He laughed, again, and agreed with me, but said he had a friend in the embassy and that may have had something to do with it. He said the tour was three years, that he was a bachelor and knew he would have a good time, and that the pressure was not as great as that of the airlift.

After absorbing the shock, I thanked him for teaching me some of the tricks, and letting me fly the bird from the left seat, knowing it would take me at least 30 flights to be able to start upgrading to the left seat, and becoming a first pilot in the MATS scheme of things. He smiled, and said he liked flying with me, because I acted aggressively, and it reminded him of himself in the early days. He went further and said I would not be able to upgrade, that it just took time, and at least three of the first pilots had to recommend the copilot for upgrading. *Quite a structured system,* I remember thinking.

We walked out to C54 43-17233, nickname Big Easy 80. We were flying a load of flour and soup, weight 20,200 pounds. There was no coal dust to contend with, just flour specks. Duty told me to get into the left seat, that he would fly the leg home. I didn't argue with him. If he had a fetish, it was about flying the home leg, and that was fine with me. I literally jumped into the left seat. The flight engineer smiled, and settled into his seat between the two pilots.

I started all four engines, for practice, and with the agreement with Duty. I triple-checked the radio compass frequency, and waited for the aircraft ahead of us, Big Easy 79, from our squadron, due for takeoff at 1457 (2:47 p.m.). He passed by our position, and we had our engines running (too early), so we sat in our position for our separation.

We "finally" got moving. Duty did not say anything, except reading the checklist. We were going to takeoff on runway 15 (to the southeast), and that was good, for we didn't have to make a long turn as we did on the first flight.

As we taxied down the taxi strip, I suddenly felt sad, for I was so used to flying with Duty, it was going to be with a different pilot after this flight. You get used to flying with the same pilot, and you both seem to meld and almost know what the other pilot is thinking. It was weird, but in future flights and, actually, in future years, this became true. I guess it was like getting married. You get used to one another, and almost become instinctive in how you think.

The airlift, besides being an experience that was never done before, and never done again on such a scale, taught one to believe one can do anything with an airplane, if one has the right people and equipment. This sounds presumptuous, after having flown two missions, but subsequent flying jobs taught the individual pilot to rely on himself, and draw from the experience we were exposed to on the Berlin affair. In retrospect, I was extremely fortunate to fly with a lot of pilots who were dedicated, and good fliers. That was obvious, from the start. Flying with the first generation of airlift pilots was an experience never to be forgotten. As a second-generation Vittles pilot, I learned what to do, and how to do it from the "old" boys. I wondered how they learned, but never got the answer.

The flight in was much the same as our previous flight. The weather was getting more cloudy, but we had been briefed that

Berlin was in good shape, weather wise, and we should have no problem getting into Templehof. The radar approach control in Berlin put us in the right position and GCA brought us in with no problem. We did have a crosswind on the final approach, and I had trouble keeping the right heading, but the radar controller was patient, and at 500 feet I looked up and saw I was in good shape. Following the lead that Duty employed on the other flight, I reduced the power, slowed another 10 knots, came over the apartment house, pushed the stick forward, rounded out a little high, and started to float. Duty said he was opening the cowl flaps (that cooled the engines), and I held the aircraft altitude, and the floating stopped. I made a safe landing, but a little hard, some 2,000 feet down the runway. I had the throttles in idle, and started braking, but had no trouble stopping, being careful not to put excessive wear on the tires. At about 60 mph I applied more brakes, and used the nose steering to get near the final taxiway, into the ramp area. Duty didn't say a word, but had a smile on his face.

After we parked, and shut down the engines, we got out of the pilot's door, down the ladder, and got a cup of coffee from the ever-present Red Cross vehicle. Duty headed back to the bird, sat down, and told me not to worry about the landing. It happened to everyone. I asked him about the cowl flaps, and he said he got that trick from an older pilot. He went on to say that the only problem was I didn't reduce the throttles enough and didn't steepen my nose-down altitude. Otherwise, my control was good, not overpowering, and I shouldn't worry. Most of the pilots who were starting out had a lot more problems than I did. With that being said, he lit up a cigarette, and walked around the aircraft, smoking and drinking his coffee, stretching his legs. This was to be the last time, and he wanted to remember it.

I called the tower, and confirmed our takeoff time as 1800 (6:00 p.m.). It was dark, but not black as I expected. Duty told me to start the engines, for practice, as he stared through the front cockpit windows. After all four engines were turning, I asked the tower for permission to taxi, after the aircraft ahead of us was already on the taxiway. We were told to taxi, and Duty increased power, and turned out onto the long taxiway. The taxiway lights were on, and I could see the runway lights on my right. We were cleared for takeoff, and Duty handled the aircraft like the veteran he was, starting our climb to 7,000 feet. We had an overcast. Duty said the overcast would be above us, and not to worry. I had tuned in the Berlin Radio beacon, and he tracked outbound to Hannover, 55 minutes away. We had our riding light on, and I could see the aircraft ahead of us, in the distance. There was no haze normally associated with West Germany. As we got within 20 minutes of Hannover, I turned in the beacon, and we were right on course. Duty patted himself on the head. It was starting to get a bit turbulent, indicating the clouds had lowered. We had no autopilot, so we had to fly the bird by hand. The reason for this was two-fold: our flights were not too long and we needed to stay sharp, and we didn't have any autopilot specialists. That seemed strange, but was told they were in short supply, and, even with our obvious priority, had to be held for long flights, whatever that meant.

We arrived over Hannover one minute late, and he turned south to Rhein-Main. He told me to fly the bird, until we got into descent range, and he would make the approach and landing. Said he wanted something to remember, on his last flight.

At 7:35 p.m. I called Frankfurt approach, and got permission to descent to 2,000 feet, for a straight in approach to runway 15. Duty took control of the aircraft, advanced the RPMs to 2,200, had me put the fuel controls into auto-rich, and reduced the manifold pressure to 20 inches, lowering the nose. I had tuned in the Rhein-Main beacon, and we were right on course. I could see the aircraft ahead of us, his tail light blinking. We looked to be in good shape. He saw the airplane ahead, and continued, deciding he was at the right distance.

"Gear down, flaps 50%, standby for landing." Duty was getting set for landing. GCA cleared us, and kept giving us headings and altitudes until we were at 500 feet, then cleared us to land. I noted that the aircraft ahead of us was turning off the runway, its landing lights clearly showing.

We landed, and turned off the runway, onto the taxiway back to our parking area. I noticed the aircraft behind us was just touching down. When we got up to the parking area, the ground crewman motioned us with hand-held lights. When he signaled with a light across his throat, we shut down the engines, and completed the checklist. The time was 1950 (7:50 p.m.). Flight time was two hours and 10 minutes.

We trudged back to the Operations. Duty got in a staff car (that was strange, but I found out later it was customary to give the pilot completing his tour a ride back to his barracks, alone. When I got inside, I noted I was to fly at 1800 (6:00 p.m.) the next day with a Captain Hudson. As usual, I never heard of him, or any of the others, for that matter. Very formal.

I went outside and got into the mini bus. There were two other crews (four pilots) and we got out of there. The driver knew what his cargo was, and spared nothing to get us back to the housing area. He pulled up at the drop-off point after only 40 minutes (a record), and I stepped out with my small bag, and wearily climbed the stairs into my barracks. I went immediately into my room, sat down on the bed, unlaced my boots, and flopped onto the bed, squiggled my toes, and drifted off to an immediate sleep. I was a lot more tired than I thought.

It was 11:30 a.m. March 3, and I struggled to get awake. I got up, put on my slippers, went down to the washroom, and washed my face, combed my hair, and got back to my room. I kept on the flying suit I had worn yesterday, put on my boots, and walked the block to the mess hall. It was fairly crowded, but after a short wait, I got my tray full of meatloaf, cabbage, sausages (German-style), fried potatoes (fried too crisp), cherry cobbler, and coffee. I drank the coffee before I got to an empty table, and went back for another one. I guess you could say I was addicted, but it helped me clear my head. I had really slept hard.

When I got to the barracks, I stripped my clothes, laid them in a bundle on the end of the bed, and went to the shower room, and plunged into the hot water, luxuriating in the warmth and relaxing feeling that came over me. I obviously was not prepared for the constant pressure, one that did not diminish after each flight. Knowing we had two flights per day didn't cause us to not be prepared for the long days.

I shaved, and got myself ready for the rest of the day. The laundry was taken care of by three maids, that cost each of us 50 pfennigs per month. That was cheap, and I found their work was outstanding. It was another way of helping the economy. Full time jobs for the West German women were not too prevalent. They were less than those of the male population. We were glad to have them, and rarely saw them. Mainly they worked in the early evening until late in the next day.

I was beginning to relax, and planned on catching the three o'clock bus to the squadron. I wrote a note to my mother, in San Francisco, didn't say much other than I had arrived and already had twenty missions under my belt. The time went by so fast it was difficult to realize what was going on. It had to be in an established routine, for I knew that was the way I had to handle the pressure. Everyone else seemed to be able to do it, so I realized that it was the daily routine that had to be set in motion. At 3:00 p.m. I got into the bus with six other pilots, and we headed for the flight line at Rhein-Main, arriving there at 3:45 p.m. I went into the operations room, and saw several pilots sitting around, obviously waiting for their flights.

I looked at the briefing board, and confirmed we were to fly at 1800 with Hudson, carrying lead weights and sandpaper (that was a strange combination, but I would realize there were no surprises in this operation). A young pilot sitting in front looked at me, stood up and extended his hand. "Dick Hudson," and I reciprocated. We sat down, and he asked how many flights I had accomplished, and when I said twenty, he smiled and said he was glad this was not my first flight. He asked me who I had flown with, and I told him. He smiled, and said I must be someone special to have flown with Duty on his last flights. That made me feel good. Then we walked out to the plane, and the flight engineer said the plane was ready to go, and added it had 15 hours before inspection. That was something new, but informative. I walked around the bird, and Hudson climbed the steps and went into the cockpit. When I got aboard, I took the cargo inspection, and found the sandpaper was in large rolls, and the lead weights were in 200 round packages. This meant it would take a little longer to offload, whatever that meant.

As I approached the cockpit, I noted Hudson was in the left seat, which I expected. He called for the checklist, even though he must have known it by heart. I surmised he had plenty of flights, at least 50, because MATS set a standard of at least 30-40 flights as a copilot before upgrading. I found they were very structured in the way they did things.

Without being told, I called the tower and asked them to confirm our takeoff time as 1800. Hudson looked at me, but said nothing. The time was confirmed, using runway 15, altimeter was 29.84. Hudson nodded, and reset his altimeter, as did I. While Hudson started the engines, I tuned the radio beacon to Darmstadt, and the homing needle pointed to 150. When the four engines had been started, Hudson called the tower and received permission to taxi. The time was 1750 (5:50 p.m.). It was getting dark, and I turned on the wing and taillights. Hudson turned on the taxi lights, and we headed toward the takeoff area.

As we approached the runway, the flight engineer said that our cargo weight was 20,500 (500 pounds over the recommended weight for takeoff). Hudson said nothing. I was to find out being over-weight as much as 1,500 pounds was nothing out of the ordinary. The tower confirmed our altimeter setting as 29.84, told us we would have a crosswind of 15 mph on takeoff, and were cleared for take-off. The windsock at the side of the runway showed the wind was brisk, and, indeed, presented a crosswind and we would see how Hudson handled this one.

The lowering of the barometric pressure, coupled with the increased wind meant, for certainty, a front was coming from the northwest. This meant within the next 24 hours Rhein-Main would be in trouble weather-wise, but Berlin should hold in good shape for 48 hours. At least, that is what I reckoned. Hudson got us clearance to take the runway and takeoff. The time was 1801. After takeoff, and climbing, Hudson started to home in on the Darmstadt beacon. The aircraft ahead of us called in at 1815. Hudson leveled off at 6,000 feet, and kept the speed at 160, to make up the minute we needed, being as our takeoff was one minute late. We were to hold our altitude. One good thing, the Russians did not like to fly at night, and definitely didn't like to fly in bad weather. Just a thought, but in as much as I had not seen a Russian MIG I couldn't divert my attention to them, under those circumstances.

Hudson kept up the airspeed, and we turned over Aschaffenburg at 1836, having made up the one minute we needed. Later I dis-cussed this with the pilot and he said that a minute here and a minute there and it all mounted up. Also, he said it was easier to get the minute back early on, rather than have the aircraft behind us have a problem with making it up.

The flight into Templehof was bumpy, but Hudson was flying the bird, and I just watched the instruments, and looked outside occasionally. The GCA controller had problems keeping us on the centerline, and had us make at least five course corrections before we were at 500 feet, and Hudson took over, and landed the airplane about 2,000 feet down the runway. It was raining slightly but had no problem taxiing. We pulled up behind the aircraft ahead of us. I noticed there were at least six C54s ahead of us, and it appeared we would have a long wait to get off the ground.

When we had completed the engine shutdown, Hudson said he was going to stay in the airplane, and I should go on out and stretch my legs and get something to eat. I didn't ask why, but got out of the plane, had a cup of coffee and a couple of donuts. It was getting windy, so I sheltered myself against the main gear, and noticed there now were four C54s in line ahead of us. It was 8:45 p.m., and I tried to compute when we would takeoff, if there was no holdup. I figured 2200, so we had some time to go. So I walked into Operations, a five-minute walk, just to see what was going on.

The inside of Templehof was a large room, partitioned off, and had a transportation desk, for people who wanted to get to Frankfurt. There was always plenty of room, and, surprisingly, there was no waiting. It was obvious, now, when I thought about it. There was a small cafeteria, and seating for about 20 people. It looked as if the big boys wanted to provide space for those who were stationed in Berlin to get back to the American Zone, or for those who wanted to go from Frankfurt or Wiesbaden, to go to Berlin, to enjoy the sights, particularly on their days off.

At 9:20 p.m. I walked back to our aircraft (Big Willie 87) and climbed the ladder to the fuselage. It was empty, and cleaned out. I went forward to the cockpit, and Hudson was on one of the bunks, taking a nap. I climbed into the right seat, turned on the power, listened to the radio for a few minutes, then contacted Departure Control, and asked for our takeoff time. They answered, saying our time was 2200 (10:00 p.m.). My guess was good. The flight engineer had been listening, and shook Hudson and he sat up in the bunk, looking at his watch. It was now 9:30 p.m., so we still had plenty of time. He patted me on the back, and slid into the left seat. We were ready to go.

Engine start, taxi and runup was normal, but the tower cautioned us that there was a 20-knot crosswind, and that the previous crews cautioned the tower to assure the pilots were aware. Our takeoff was okay, but Hudson had to use a lot of aileron to keep the aircraft on the center of the runway. He called for gear up, flaps up, and change the power during our climb.

The final approach to Templehof. May 1949. Note the fog and hazards of buildings on the approach.

Chapter Eight
WEATHER COMPLICATIONS

The trip back was routine, but we were encountering tur
bulence at 7,000 feet, and had a pretty good headwind,
that added about five minutes on our leg from Berlin to
Hannover. Hudson had about a 10-degree change in heading to
maintain the proper course from Hannover to Frankfurt. As we
approached Rhein-Main, I contacted Approach Control, and was
advised there was rain in the area, and visibility was down to one
mile, with a strong crosswind from the west (right as we approached). We were cleared to descend to 2,000 feet, and handed
off to GCA, who immediately turned us five degrees right (obviously to correct for the wind from the west).

We descended to 2,000 feet, and was told we were approaching
the glide path (three miles from the runway) and to prepare for
some turbulence. At the same moment, the aircraft shook and then
slowed to the left. GCA immediately recognized this and changed
our heading five degrees to the right. Hudson was really fighting
the turbulence, and as we reached the glide path, he called for half
flaps (full flaps is normal for the C54). I dropped half flaps, and
confirmed the gear was down and locked. I advised him I was standing by with the windshield wipers, and he confirmed this, but to
hold the landing lights. He didn't want to be blinded by the rain
and the glare of the lights.

GCA advised us we were approaching 500 feet, and, if we had
the runway in sight, to take over and land the aircraft. I told Hudson
I had the approach lights (high intensity strobe lights), and he took
over visually, with a 10-degree correction as directed by GCA to
eliminate the harsh crosswind. As he started to the round out, he
called for landing lights, kicked the rudder to align himself with
the runway heading, and compensated for this wind correction by
cranking in aileron. He touched down right landing gear first, then
let the airplane settle on the left side of the runway. We started
braking immediately, keeping the aileron in. Hudson did not want
to use the nosewheel steering if the nose was canted into the wind.

If you did this, with a crab (nose off center) the nosewheel would really cause us to start a turn long before the speed was slow enough. This was learned only after many landings of the C54, and they didn't teach this in the flight school at Great Falls. That is because the instructors, for the main part, were used to landing the C47, that did not have tricycle gear.

Hudson said he was exhausted, and he looked it. The back of his flying suit was soaked, even though it was 5:50 a.m. I wasn't feeling too good myself. I wasn't used to these early hours, and then to have to go again. Hudson asked me if I thought I could make it around the horn, and I responded, by saying I had learned a lot from him, and would make it okay. We were agreed to my flying, so we sat down, and I relaxed, as much as I could. Hudson had enough time in that he dropped off into a nap, without hardly any problem. We were scheduled for our next takeoff at 7:00 a.m., so we had the time to relax. I decided to go outside, and get some fresh air, even though the wind was really blowing hard.

The wind swept the flight line and was very invigorating. One of our squadron airplanes taxied by, and waved at me. I waved back and clasped my hands. The pilot gave me a "thumbs up," and that made me feel good. After about 10 minutes, I returned inside and went to the bathroom, and stopped by the canteen to get a cup of coffee, and two sugarcoated rolls. That perked me up and I almost felt as if I was ready to go again. We had a 0700 takeoff, with the same aircraft (that was kind of a shock, but the time involved from our landing to our next takeoff, plus the fact the coal flatbed was waiting for us. That was a surprise!

At 6:40 a.m. I shook Hudson, and he went into the bathroom, and washed his face, and came back with a smile on his face. He said he had flown five days in a row, and it was beginning to get to him. The start up, taxi out, and getting on the runway was no problem. As I increased the throttles, the aircraft started to drift to the right, as a consequence of the crosswind from our right. I didn't anticipate it to catch hold this early, but cranked in the aileron, and stabilized the nose. The takeoff was okay, but I had to crank in more correction. We ran into quite a bit of turbulence, and clouds, at about 3,000 feet, but was in the clear at 6,000 feet. It was captivating to look down and see a blanket of white in the early morning.

We arrived at Templehof at about 9:00 a.m., and the weather was scheduled for low clouds, gusting winds and rain off and on. Everything was okay until they turned us onto the final approach. GCA had trouble keeping us on the centerline, but finally settled down, and we made a good approach. Following Hudson's lead onto the first flight, I dropped half flaps, making control easier, even with the full load of cargo. At 400 feet I saw runway lights, slowed the aircraft by 10 mph, and dropped the nose and aimed at the end of the runway. It always seemed as though we were going to skim the tops of the apartment buildings, but we cleared them, and landed about 1,500 feet down the runway. The wind was directly on our nose, so slowing down was no problem. The wind at Templehof was tricky. You never knew how it was going to be but you get used to the changes. I asked Hudson about landing to the east, and he said he never had to use that runway. Strange.

There were five aircraft ahead of us, to takeoff, so we had some time before we had to get going. Five C54s at three-minute intervals was 15 minutes, plus 10 minutes for start up and taxi made it 25 minutes. Our takeoff was scheduled for 10:15 a.m., so we had to start engines at 0950. Things on the airlift were based on timing, and you had to mentally position yourself so you were not early or late. It sounded easy, but actually too many things could happen, but we learned you always plan for an emergency. If something happened to change your takeoff, you advised the tower, and they would tell you to be ready when you could, and they would reschedule you for another takeoff time. They were in control all the time. I didn't know until later that a Vittles-qualified pilot was in the tower, and made some quick decisions, based on his expertise. It worked, so our schedule seemed to fit into the scheme, but, again, everything had to work out right, and usually did.

We followed the C54 ahead of us after he had taxied out to the takeoff spot. I checked the Templehof beacon, and the wing-tail lights. The landing lights were on, and the flight engineer climbed back into his seat, and told me the cargo had been emptied, and we were light. Some of the flight engineers did that, but some did not.

The takeoff was normal, but we hit turbulence when we cleared the west perimeter of the operations building. I climbed to 7,000 feet and throttled back, adjusting the RPMs, and trimmed the aircraft, but it wasn't easy, for the turbulence was bouncing us around. I let the bumps keep us straight and level, and didn't try to correct to each and every waver. I learned early that you couldn't fight the weather, or you would exhaust yourself in an hour. Hudson actually was sitting back with his head on the seat back, and looked like he was taking another nap. I had my hands full, and couldn't watch him and the aircraft. The flight engineer had left his seat, and was taking a nap on one of the bunks. I felt completely alone, and that was okay, even though I was on my fourth flight, a real rookie, so to speak.

The flight from Berlin to Hannover was seven minutes longer than I planned. The wind was coming right at us, and was getting pretty rough. When we turned over Hannover, and started our final leg to Frankfurt, I was blown off course pretty fast, but we were in the American Zone, so I corrected after I let the wind blow us off course. The correction I made was 15 degrees, pretty extreme, but it got us back on the correct course, after five minutes. I held the correction until the compass showed us on course, and then I corrected us back. That kept us on course, and I tuned in the Rhein-Main radio beacon, and had to correct to the right, again. This wind must be a lulu, I remember thinking, as I corrected once again. As we got close enough, I called Approach Control, and was cleared to 2,000 feet, and expect a radar approach. They told me it was very turbulent at lower altitudes, and to expect a crosswind on the final approach.

On the approach, I lowered the gear and half flaps, and followed GCA instructions. He had trouble with the wind shear, and kept correcting me to the right, on the was to runway 15. We went through the clouds at 1,200 feet, and the bird shook, and flopped left and right, but I let it go, and stayed on my heading and altitude, although the descent of 500 feet per minute was not easy. The plane just didn't want to settle down, so, uncharacteristically, I fought the controls. At 500 feet I saw the strobe lights, and disregarding GCA, maneuvered the aircraft on the final half mile to the runway.

It got easier, and I stopped fighting the controls, and kept the nose straight, using both rudder and aileron.

We touched down about 2,000 feet (I let the airspeed build up, because it was easier to combat the wind problem) and landed okay, but kicked out the rudder and used strictly aileron. We skipped, and then settled down on the runway. I got it under control, and turned off at the far end, and taxied back, tired, but satisfied. Hudson said nothing, but said we had two days off, and he would see me on the third day. I found out later he had asked for me to fly with him, and operations did so for the next 22 flights.

Inside the underhange of the Operations/Maintenance Building at Templehof. It was built to protect the planes and passengers from inclement weather. It was very awesome. March 1949.

Chapter Nine

EMERGENCY

We were back in the air on February 24, and the next 15 flights went by fairly easily, except the weather was getting progressively worse at both Rhein-Main and Templehof. On March 9, I was flying the left seat, with Hudson in the copilot's position, and the flight into Templehof was routine, with a small amount of rain. On the flight back, at night, we had taken off, got the gear and flaps up, when a shock hit me. Our number one engine was on fire, and it lit up the cockpit like a flare. It almost was like the time in 1944 when a piece of flak hit us in the nose of the B17, and bounced all over the nose compartment. This was different, because I had to control the airplane. I corrected the low wing altitude, feathered the left engine and pulled the fire button (shot fire retardant into the engine), pulled the throttle back, and put the fuel control valve into cutoff. Hudson was calling Departure Control, and asked them for immediate landing. Departure Control put us in touch with Gatow arrival, who switched us over to Gatow approach, following GCA instructions.

I was level at 2,000 feet. They told me I was on a short final approach. I dropped the gear, lowered half flaps, then trimmed the aircraft for a three-engine landing. Gatow told me to start descent at 1,000 feet per minute, that I was high on the glide path. I complied, and at 500 feet, they told me to resume normal glide posture. I saw the runway, switched on the landing lights, and was cleared to land. The fire trucks were waiting on the far end of the runway, with their lights flashing. Hudson opened the cowl flaps, and we landed kind of hard, but it was on the ground. For some unknown reason, I thanked GCA right then and there. They "rogered," and cleared us to the ramp.

Things occurred so quickly, I acted by instinct, and did everything right, fortunately. Hudson said, when we got out of the aircraft, he had never seen such a young C54 pilot react so fast, that I didn't take the time to think, and that is the way you're taught. He just shook his head, and got in the back of the jeep, and still didn't think of what had happened. When we got in Gatow Operations, the operations officer told us we could fly back with the Navy. We were going to go back to Rhein-Main with a VR-6 crew. It was due to leave in about 30 minutes. He said we just had time for a cup of coffee. Its too bad we landed at night, for I thought, later, it would be nice to see what another Berlin airbase looked like.

We got a ride out to the VR6 airplane (a Navy C54), and climbed aboard. The pilots motioned us up to the front end, and one of them yelled to relax on the bunks, and they would get us home. We did just that, and the flight back was rough, but I finally learned why the Navy flew more missions than the Air Force did, consequently got more tonnage per day. They flew the trip back at 190 mph, and they were manhandling the aircraft and disregarded the limitations of the C54. They flew like we never thought we were supposed to fly the C54, by exceeding the airspeed limitations, and manhandled it, all the way to the ground. They disregarded the time limitations of the flight back to Rhein-Main, gaining several minutes to get the plane recycled for the second flight. It was truly amazing, but I wondered what the maintenance schedule looked like.

Hudson and I discussed this return flight, and came to the conclusion that the Navy exceeded the Air Force tonnage by flying faster, and their turnaround was much quicker than ours. We went back to our operations building, and found that we were scheduled for March 14, for our next two flights. It didn't turn out that way, for Hudson had a throat virus, and was grounded until the flight surgeon could get it under control. In the meantime, a Captain John Rushlau took the place of Hudson. I had met John in the mess hall, and he was a short, lean pilot, who lived off base, and drove his own car, a Belgian Ford (that looked like an American model, but was built in Brussels). I remember thinking, this guy must have an outside income. He even had an American girlfriend, a stewardess for one of the commercial airlines flying into Frankfurt.

We were to fly another late night mission, so I got some sleep, and finally got my ears clear, after the antics of the Navy. Fortunately, I never had ear blockage until last night. My ears were sore for two days, but presented no problems. The flights were routine. Rushlau was a good pilot, and we split the left seat time. The weather stayed the same, and I was thankful for the GCA operators. We used the radar approach on both landings, but we at least were not confronted with the crosswinds we had on the previous flights. We didn't worry about getting in, even when the ceiling was below 500 feet, a feat we never could have tried back home, unless the priority warranted it. Before GCA we had to depend on the radio compass and the capability of each pilot. The new innovation of radar was a godsend to us, and the efficiency of the pilots and mission requirements zoomed.

On March 22, on my scheduled 33rd flight, I was scheduled to take a C54 to Burtonwood, England, that was, I found out, the maintenance depot for the Skymasters. They were sure busy, getting the birds from four bases back into good flying condition. This included changing all four engines, testing all the other equipment, including a new radio for talking with the ground. The tires were changed, and the bird was pressure-cleaned, to get rid of all the coal dust that had accumulated over the last 50 flights. It came out spotless, and took the better part of three days. We test-hopped (to make sure the plane was airworthy, and everything worked as it should). We landed, gave the aircraft our okay, and flew for Rhein-Main the same day.

The flight was routine, but we had some bumpy weather on the way back over the channel. The pilot, Captain Jim Nelson, flew it back, and I just watched the scenery, when I could see it. England had not changed. It looked the same as it had four years ago. Burtonwood was in the southwest part of the island. Nice, flat country. It always seemed green.

A ramp view of Templehof Air Base, West Berlin. Note the Operations building in the background, and the C-54s in the foreground. May 1949.

Chapter Ten
THE UPGRADING

After returning to Rhein-Main, I flew 19 more airlift flights, with different pilots, and everything was getting to be routine. No emergencies, no problems. The number of flights and total amounts of flying time kept building up, and we all got tired after the fifth flight on each cycle. I had been flying mostly at night, and noticed the new pilots were coming out of Great Falls in large numbers, out matching those who had completed their tour of 100 flights leaving for other assignments. Mostly in MATS, I noticed. A closed corporation, I remember thinking. Well, with all that experience, it seemed logical to do it this way. MATS was playing an ever-increasing part in the Air Force system. The Strategic Air Command had not made its appearance. This would happen in the early part of 1950.

I had 48 flights behind me, and was considered more-or-less of an old hand. I had expected to get upgraded to a qualified MATS first pilot in the next few flights.

As we returned from our last early morning flight, the weather had turned chilly, and we hurried into Operations. The new flight schedule was posted and I had three days off, then was scheduled for my first upgrading flight, with a Captain Pruyne. I hurried out to the mini-bus, and then it sunk in. I was finally going to become a first pilot, in MATS. Some of the younger pilots were satisfied to stay in the copilot's slot, but not me. John Rushlau was on the bus (his Ford was in the shop), and I asked him about Pruyne. He smiled, and rubbed my back. John and I had gotten to be good friends. He was from Denver, and his parents ran a snow resort in the Rockies. He was an accomplished skier, and had gone to Garmish, West Germany, several times on his days off (MATS had a resort "special" flight that went to the Garmiksh-Belkenkirchen airport once a week).

Luther Pruyne was of German descent. His folks still lived in a small town south of Munich. He participated in the C47 operations in the latter part of World War II and flew some of the first Airlift missions in the C47, then transferred to Rhein-Main (from Wiesbaden) and completed his tour several months ago. He was a bachelor, and requested to stay in Frankfurt, and became a line instructor (one of the best, according to Rushlau) and flew with all three squadrons of the 513th, acting as a senior check pilot. This seemed very good to me, for I wanted to get a real impression of my capability, and this guy sounded like he knew it all. Good. My first upgrading flight was to take place on April 12, with an early takeoff time in the afternoon. Our second flight should be in the late evening, and that was fine, for I liked flying at night.

The airplane was C54 42-72615, load was 20,680 pounds of coal, call sign Big Easy 85. We were scheduled for a 3:00 p.m. takeoff, and I showed up at 1:00 p.m., for I fully expected a long briefing, by Pruyne, on what I was expected to do, when, etc. He showed up at 1:30 p.m., introduced himself, and said this was going to be my first upgrading flight. He asked me how many airlift flights I had (he already knew), and noted I had graduated from the Great Falls flights. He asked me what I thought of those preliminary flights, and I quite frankly told him that, other than the GCAs and the courseline indicator procedure, I enjoyed flying the C54. He nodded, made some notes, and said we should get a cup of coffee, confirm our takeoff from the Operations desk (I had not done this before); it surely saved some time.

Operations confirmed us as Big Easy 85, with our initial takeoff confirmed as 1500. At 2:35 p.m., we went out to our airplane. The flight engineer was waiting for us, and said the bird was ready, and had 40 hours until the next inspection. I found out from Pruyne, that knowledge of the time remaining until the next inspection was a learned experience, and kept the flight crews aware of how the aircraft would function, and more importantly, was there any previous repeat problems. Good to know.

Pruyne reiterated he would read the checklist, and do what I told him, but only after I asked. I nodded, and started the engines. I told him to call the tower and confirm our takeoff time, which he did, and confirmed 3:00 p.m. The taxi out, takeoff, and climb on course; the takeoff runway was 15, homing in on the Damstadt beacon. On to Aschaffenburg, I called for him to tune in Aschaffenburg. He did, and I settled down, adjusted the manifold and engine RPM, trimmed the aircraft, and tried to relax. It seemed he was constantly writing. This disconcerted me, temporarily, but I soon forgot and concentrated on flying the airplane.

"Big Easy 66, Fulda at :11." The call startled me, and I noted our scheduled Fulda time was 1614, so we had no adjustments. As we turned on course from Fulda to Berlin, I called out, "Big Easy 85, Fulda at :14." I thought I should have had Pruyne make the call, but that was that. I had trouble lining up the courseline indicator, having to correct to the right several times. After about ten minutes I settled the course down. Pruyne leaned over, and said to check the smoke on the ground, and I would find a strong wind from the right. Then he smiled and wrote, again.

I told him to call Approach, and request descent and approach to Templehof. We were told to descend to 3,000 feet, we were number three for approach. Altimeter 29.82. Weather at Templehof was 500 feet and one mile, in fog and rain. Pruyne didn't say anything. I leveled out at 3,000 feet, adjusted the power, retrimmed, and waited for the next transmission. It wasn't long in coming. The weather was at our altitude, and the turbulence was sporadic. We were told to turn left to 350 degrees, and descend to 2,000 feet, that this was our extended base leg. I retarded the throttles, adjusted the RPM, and got down to 2,000 feet without any trouble. I called for the gear down, and the flaps to 50%. Pruyne did everything I told him, and confirmed the gear was down and locked.

GCA turned us left to 270 degrees. He told us the turn put us right on the centerline, and we were one-quarter mile from glide path. I double-checked the power, fuel controls, gear and flaps, and we were ready to land. Pruyne just sat there. I retrimmed the aircraft, and GCA told us to start our descent, at 500 feet per minute, on course and on centerline. The clouds kept us from seeing the runway, but we were still going through 1,000 feet, the approach speed was 120 mph. Everything was under control.

At 400 feet I saw the runway lights, and went over the apartment house with space to spare, rounded out, and touched down at the usual 1,500 feet. I started light braking, and when we got near the taxiway, I put more pressure on the brakes, told Pruyne to open the cowl flaps, and started my turn with the nosewheel steering engaged.

The landing was okay, and the post-flight was satisfactory. There were five aircraft ahead of us, and I asked Pruyne if he had no problem, I was going to leave the bird and get some coffee and donuts. He nodded, and started writing, again. It was getting disconcerting.

As I approached the Red Cross truck, I saw John Rushlau, and he waved to me. I came up, shook his hand, and asked him how he was doing. He said he had a new pilot on his third flight, and quite frankly, he looked scared to death. The new pilot stood a discreet distance from us. John asked how I was doing, and I told him I had no major mistakes, but Pruyne was always writing. John laughed, and asked if Pruyne said anything, and I said "no," and he said this was good. If Pruyne had something to say, you would know it, so consider I passed the first upgrading mission. That made me feel good. John said he had to get back, that the startup was going to take more time than he expected, and so he wanted to be ready, and make his takeoff time on schedule. I waved to him as he climbed into the aircraft ahead of us.

As I got into the pilots compartment, Pruyne opened his eyes, waved, and said he was ready. We had several minutes before our time, so I took my time to get into the seat, strap in, and check the controls, then I called for the before start engines checklist. The taxi and takeoff was normal, and we got into the clouds at 1,000 feet, and it got bumpy and was not easy to control. The flight back was normal, and Pruyne didn't have much to write down, so I just flew the bird. I called over Hannover, turned on course, and flew towards Frankfurt.

As we approached the base, I called Approach and asked for permission to descend, and was told to descend to 2,000 feet, altimeter was 29.90, wind from the southeast at ten mph, and we were number three for landing. I told Pruyne to confirm, and reduced power, increased the RPMs, put the fuel controls in maximum, and started a 500 foot per minute, rounding out at 2,000 feet, and told Pruyne to call in. He did so, and we were cleared to GCA. The approach and landing were normal, we broke out at 800 feet, and I saw the strobe lights slightly to the left, corrected, and the landing was okay. Our taxi back was normal.

Our second flight was scheduled for 2100 (9:00 p.m.). We were to fly the second flight in the same aircraft. Big Easy 85. The weather was not too good. The wind was gusty, but generally from the southeast, and using runway 15 made it a lot easier, for the reasons stated before.

Pruyne had me sit down in the briefing room, and gave me a short critique, saying that I was doing fine, that my procedures were very good, and my control of the aircraft was excellent. The next flight should be the determining factor, and he didn't anticipate any problems. Our takeoff was to be on time, according to the operations specialist, and we went to the bathroom, and walked out to the aircraft. It was the third plane down the row from our operations building. As we approached, the offloading crew was removing the cargo ramp, and the flight engineer was about to close the twin cargo doors. He saw us, and waved, giving Pruyne a "thumbs up."

I called the tower, and was confirmed as having a 2100 takeoff. At ten minutes to 9:00 p.m., I called for start engines, and we went through the checklist without any problems. I told Pruyne to tune in and identify the Darmstadt beacon, and he confirmed it. The C54 ahead of us taxied by, with a big 78 painted on the tail. All C54s had a permanent Big Easy/Willie call sign, and it was painted on the tail with huge black numbers. It was easy to read from at least a mile away.

The taxi out and takeoff was normal. The wind had died down, and I had no problem getting the nose off the ground, and the takeoff was better than normal, for me. I set course for Darmstadt. We ran into low clouds at Aschaffenburg, and when we got to Fulda (the entry into the Russian Zone), we were one minute early, so I turned on course, announcing to anyone that Big Easy 85 was over Fulda (they knew I was one minute early). I slowed down five mph, held it for ten minutes, then resumed the 150 mph. Tracking outbound was not a problem. Wind gave me no trouble, and I held the proper heading all the way in. Pruyne had said nothing.

When within range, I called Rhein-Main Approach Control, and asked permission to descend to 2,000 feet, and was told to hold for two minutes, then start down. I agreed and complied. When reaching 2,000 feet, Approach Control told us the weather was deteriorating, now was 400 feet with one-mile visibility. There was no change in Pruynes' look, and he didn't write anything down, so I assumed we were in good shape. About that time, Approach called and told us to turn left to 350 and drop our gear and flaps. I dropped the gear, lowered 50% flaps, retrimmed the aircraft after resetting the engine power, and holding the manifold pressure (throttles). GCA came on the air, and told us to turn left to 290 degrees, and said we were four miles from touchdown. It seemed they had turned us in close, probably because of the weather. Heading was good, and GCA told us to check our gear and flaps, and to start our descent at 500 feet per minute. We settled down on the glide path. GCA said we were ten feet high, and increase our rate of descent. Pruyne said not to worry. Sometimes the GCA operator was slow to correct our height.

As we passed through 700 feet, GCA said we were on course, and to resume normal rate of descent (500 feet per minute). I eased back on the controls, and settled down on the proper rate of descent. The clouds were getting thinner, and, at 400 feet, I saw the runway lights. It was raining, and I was right on course. As we passed over the apartments, I took over visually and dropped the nose, retarded the throttles, and for the first time, lowered full flaps. Pruyne nodded, and said, later, most of the new pilots forget to lower full flaps under weather conditions. Ok so far, I thought.

After we shut down the engines, I didn't get out of my seat, but asked Pruyne about the radar approach. He said not to worry. He could always tell when there was a new GCA controller, that their voice pitch was higher than the old boys. He also said the newer ones rushed their instructions, and this sometimes got the pilots to become tense, but, he said, I was not one of those. He also suggested if I got some time off, I should become acquainted with the radar truck at Templehof, so I could understand how they operated, and meet some of the operators. He said I would be surprised at the age of most of them. They were old timers at the age of 30, and their tour was as tough as it gets. I thanked him, and asked if he wanted me to bring him coffee and a donut, and he declined, saying, quite frankly, when we got out of Berlin he was going to take a nap in one of the bunks. That was a real shock, for I thought he would keep the pressure on me, and I probably would have to fly one more round trip, but we'd have to see, after what Pruyne said, in revelation.

After it was all over, I have thought of Luther Pruyne with a genuine admiration (I am not one who gives plaudits, except in rare cases). He taught me how to think, how to fly, and generally how to handle myself in emergency conditions, even though we had no tense situations, except maybe the radar approached and landings.

We were programmed for takeoff at 2110 (9:10 p.m.). It was raining, and the cloud layer was about 400 feet. There was no wind to speak of, so we should have no problems with our takeoff. We took off on time, and the climb out was without problems, but we had some small turbulence when we came out of the clouds at 5,000 feet, and leveling off at our altitude, it was dark but the stars were out, and it was very pretty. Pruyne tapped me on the shoulder, and said he was going to take a nap, and to wake him when we were ready to make our approach at Frankfurt. The flight engineer got out of his seat, to make way for the pilot, and squeezed my arm. He was in his late 30's and, when Pruyne had settled himself, the flight engineer got into his seat, and smiled, saying, unofficially, I had it made, and just don't screw up the landing. With that, he closed his eyes, sat back in his seat, and appeared to take a nap.

The flight was of little consequence, and, at 70 miles from Rhein-Main I called Approach, and asked permission to start down, and level off at 2,000 feet. They answered, telling us to start down. The altimeter setting was 29.89, and the wind from 160 at 5 mph. The weather was 800 feet and a mile and a half, with rain. I told the flight engineer to wake Captain Pruyne, and advised him we were ready to start down. He smiled and got out of his seat. Several minutes later Pruyne got back in the right seat, and commented that this was as much sleep as he had gotten for a week. Apparently, the pressure was on the instructors, that Operations was forecasting the loss of quite a few pilots who were finishing up their tours, and we needed replacement first pilots in a hurry.

As we passed through 4,000, Approach Control asked us what our altitude was. I told them, and they said to continue to 2,000, that we were number three to land. It sounded to me as if they were getting stacked up, and hoped we would not have to go around to make space available.

We leveled off at 2,000, and advised Approach. They came back and said to do a 360 degree turn, that the next aircraft had missed his approach, and we had to hold, for spacing. A 360-degree turn is a complete revolution and ends back up at the original heading. Pruyne nodded as I completed my turn. At low altitude, the bigger aircraft, as with the C54s, were not too stable, but, with trim and power, we had little control problems. Pruyne called approach and said we had completed our turn and were ready for landing. He did not take control, and I said nothing. He was the instructor, and could do what he wanted.

"Big Willie 85, we have you on course, at 2,000 feet, prepare for landing. You are seven miles from touchdown. Confirm gear and flaps down." I confirmed, and told Pruyne to lower the gear and drop flaps. At the same time I adjusted the RPMs, and the manifold pressure, retrimmed the aircraft. "Big Willie 85 you are on glide path and heading. Start your descent, now." I reduced power, started a 500-foot per minute descent, and retrimmed the aircraft. "On course, on centerline. Weather is now 700 feet, one mile in heavy rain. Continue your approach."

"Willie 85, you should be passing 700 feet, one mile from touch-down. Continue approach. Do you have the runway in sight?" I looked up, and Pruyne nodded yes. I saw the strobes, and then the runway lights. I called for the windshield wipers, and aligned my-self to the runway. I dropped full flaps, for there was no appre-ciable wind. I turned on the landing lights, and settled the aircraft in a landing altitude. The landing was one of my better ones, and Pruyne just shook his head. The flight engineer patted me on the back. I braked, and slowed the bird. When we reached a lower speed, I started my turn to the right and turned off at the final taxiway.

Pruyne said nothing as we taxied, but he did write down some-thing on his clipboard. The ground crew was waiting for us, and we pulled in, set the parking brake, and shut down.

As we were getting ready to get off the bird, the flight engineer said the time was two hours and fifteen minutes. Pruyne and I wan-dered into operations, and Pruyne said to grab a table, he had to go to the bathroom, and have a few words with the operations officer. This was the first time I heard an officer was on duty. It made sense, for he had to make decisions, and acted like a duty officer. I leaned back in my folding chair, and closed my eyes. I had checked the flight board, and noticed, the operations clerk had changed my name to that of another pilot. That bothered me, but figured I would soon know what was going on.

The instructor came back, sat down, pounded his fist on the table (I guess to get me awake), and said , "Hell, I can't teach you anything. You are now a first pilot. Congratulations," and extended his hand. We shook hands, and he said it was good to fly with me. He asked what I had flown and how much time I had, and I told him I flew the B25 at the end of the war, and had about 1300 hours. He smiled, and said that my use of trim was uncanny, and to keep it up. He said he told the operations officer to give me a day off, and then I should be relaxed. He got up, patted me on the back, and went out. I later found out he had his own car, and lived just off the base, in a small apartment. He surely was a nice guy, and I vividly remember him, even though we only flew twice together. I appreciated the day off, for he knew how I felt, and needed to relax. For, after that, I had to start over again, but this time I was the responsible pilot, and that made a difference.

The C-54s unloading on the ramp at Templehof, january 1949.

Chapter Eleven
BEGINNING OF THE END

After April 13, my flights came and went, with a regularity that could get boring, if I didn't get so tired. Flying five days (two flights per day) and two days off, gave me no time to enjoy the area. I had to remind myself that we were there for one purpose, that is to keep the Berliners alive, in relative comfort. That statement was just words, for the people in the capital had problems we could not imagine, let alone exist under.

My first flight as a first pilot was at night, in C54 tail number 44-9129, nicknamed Big Easy/Willie 83, and we carried 20,420 pounds of coal. I believed that this was because the weather was turning colder, and the people had to stay relatively warm. The weather was all right at Frankfurt, but Berlin was low overcast, with rain, and the temperature was in the low 40s. That was very cold, by my standards. My copilot was a Lieutenant Harry Lamm, who had only three Airlift flights under his belt. I decided to fly both missions in the left seat, so he could get experience, and I would let him fly partway into Berlin, and fly to Hannover and part of the way back to our base.

I took the 9:00 p.m. minibus from our quarters, and arrived with plenty of time. When I walked in, there were several pilots clustered around the canteen, talking to the Red Cross lady. There was another tall first lieutenant sitting on one of the folding chairs. When he saw me he got up and extended his hand, and smiled. After the introductions, I came right out and asked him how many flights he had, and he said he had four, and wanted to know how many I had. I told him I had 85 and I would fly the left seat on both of our flights, but he could expect to fly the aircraft at least half of the time, and from the right seat. He didn't complain, and said he was happy to know what was going on.

Apparently, his first four missions he rode in the right seat, and didn't touch the controls. This proved to be correct, and we got more and more acquainted. He seemed nice, had no four-engine experience, and was an air training command C47 pilot, who had recently graduated from Great Falls. That was interesting, for he wanted to know how I liked the Montana training, in comparison with the "real thing."

As we were walking out to our aircraft, I said the only problem I had was with the quality of the instructors, but that couldn't be helped, for, when I went through, the airlift was in its infancy, and did not have any experienced airlift people to use for the new pilots. It seemed to me to be the best that could be expected, under the circumstances. I told Lamm he would read the checklist, and he could expect to fly from Darmstadt to Aschaffenburg, and after we got into the corridor, I would expect him to fly part of the way. He nodded in agreement.

I called for the checklist, and he read it just fine, and I called the tower to continue our programmed takeoff time as 2215 (10:15 p.m.) and they confirmed it. I noticed an aircraft on the runway, and one starting to taxi on our right, so I waited for the aircraft on the runway to start his takeoff role, and we started four engines. I took the time to explain to Lamm that this was a good way to gauge our timing. He understood what I was saying, and I hoped he filed it away in his head.

We taxied out, and the aircraft ahead of us had started his takeoff, so our timing was good. At 2215 we took the runway and took off. Lamm looked at his watch, and smiled. I told him after 80-odd flights, you had to learn something, and I laughed. The time to Darmstadt was noted, and I asked Lamm what he expected. He came back with an answer that differed only two minutes from mine, so I said nothing. We leveled off at 6,000, adjusted the power, trimmed the bird, and flew into Darmstadt. Over the turning point, I called, in the open, that Big Easy 83 was over Darmstadt at the time I anticipated. Lamm made a note of it, and I pointed to the controls, and took my hands off the controls. He grabbed them and started flying. The trip in to Berlin was uneventful, except there was a low overcast, so I couldn't show the new copilot some of the landmarks we could use if the courseline computer failed. I again stated (I'm sure it was told to him several times) that the ten mile corridor was not as big as one would think. Lamm flew the plane okay, and had to keep from wandering off course, instead of trimming the bird so he didn't constantly have to make corrections.

Upon reaching Berlin, we started the radio procedures, that were standard, and were told the altimeter setting (that was crucial) and the weather, that was 1,000 feet overcast, with two miles visibility, with light rain. I made the approach, so the copilot would get used to the way things went. I made the landing over the apartment houses, and looked at Lamm. His eyes got as big as saucers, for he still had not gotten used to the way we approached and landed at Templehof. I remember that I had the same problems with assimilating the method of approach.

After landing, we taxied to the parking area, and found the offload crew and flatbed truck were already waiting. The engine shutdown was normal. I told Lamm that we should get out of the aircraft and stretch our legs, and get a cup of coffee and donuts. He said he wanted to stay in the aircraft, and review what had gone on. I remember that things went fast, but predictable, so I agreed, and got out of the pilots door, and stretched, and had a cup off coffee and two donuts. It felt good, and I sat down by the main landing gear. We didn't have much time, so I watched until the coal had been offloaded, and swept out, then used the cargo door metal ladder, and got back in to the cockpit. Lamm was sitting there, and staring out of the front windows. He looked at me as I entered, and smiled. He reviewed what had happened.

As I climbed into the left seat, I told Lamm to start the engines while I strapped in. He turned on the aircraft power, and got the four engines started. He had trouble with the number two engine, but he didn't use enough priming to get fuel into the engines. I helped him, and we got a belch of smoke from the engine, and it got turned over. The aircraft ahead of us was at the end of the runway, so I told him to start taxiing. When he got to the taxiway, he said for me to steer the plane. I smiled. I had made the same mistake in the early days. I steered as he was checking the cockpit, and turned in the Templehof beacon, checked it, and said we were ready for takeoff. He had stopped the plane short of the runway. I had to call the tower, for takeoff clearance, and Lamm shook his head. It was something he should have done. We were cleared for takeoff.

I brought the plane onto the runway, straightened it out, and told him to takeoff. He put the power up to the stops, and started to roll.

At 90 mph he lifted the nose into a too-high position, and the aircraft staggered into the air., with the nose too high. We cleared the maintenance hangers, and he called for gear and flaps, and climbing power. I brought up the gear, zeroed the flaps, and reset the manifold pressure to its proper setting. We climbed through the clouds, and finally called Departure Control, because Lamm had forgotten. They cleared us on course (270 degrees), and Lamm started to track outbound from Berlin.

As we passed over Hannover, Lamm turned to the left, to a course of 165 degrees. I waited for a minute, and then called, in the clear, we had passed Hannover two minutes early. Lamm shook his head, knowing he had goofed again. He was having trouble maintaining his altitude, and was too preoccupied to follow his requirements.

The weather at Rhein-Main was 100 feet and three miles, and we were cleared to descend to 2,000 feet. I took control of Big Willie 85, and told Lamm to make the calls, and start the before landing checklist. He called Approach, and was told to turn left to 270 degrees, that we were on a long base leg for runway 15. We were stable at 2,000 feet, and GCA brought us right down the chute, and the landing was a good one. We taxied off the runway, and started back to the parking area.

As we pulled into our parking spot, I stopped the aircraft, using the brakes, and shut down the engines, and turned off the power. I told Lamm that we had a 0300 takeoff, for him to confirm it with the operations duty officer, while I went to the bathroom. He said nothing, knowing I was not happy with his performance.

After a cup of coffee, the time was 0200, so we had plenty of time to try to relax. I had a talk with Lamm, and told him he had to get with the program, and know what he had to do, even if I didn't say anything. He nodded, and got a cup of coffee.

The next 40 missions went by slowly, and I flew with pilots who had completed from three to 20 missions, and the quality of their performance got better. Between May and August several things happened that are worthy of note. The weather gradually got better, and the temperature slowly climbed. The Civil Engineers at Templehof completed a new runway, same headings, but the difference was the approach. It was made over a cemetery, and the first few times it was kind of disconcerting to see the graves directly in our line, but the main difference was we didn't have to dive to the runway, and the new runway was 7,000 feet long, and it sure made things a lot easier. I actually believe it speeded things up. For one thing, GCA had a straight-in approach altitude for the aircraft, and not have to worry about bouncing off the apartment houses.

General Tunner was transferred to the states, and General Cannon took over as CALTF commander, and he now had enough pilots to change the rotation from five days flying, two days off, to four and three. That sure was a blessing, even if it came late in the campaign.

With the weather clearing up, the Russians decided to buzz us in the corridor, and had a lot of fun doing it. Most of the time they came straight at us but other times they would come for the rear, and once one of them even flew formation with us for about five minutes. I was flying the left seat, and the MIG 15 was on our left wing. I looked at him, and he looked at us. I finally waved, and he just dived away. The radio chatter from the Airlift planes was pathetic. Most of our pilots had not fought in the Eighth Air Force from England, and they got a little panicky, but it just made me chuckle.

After a couple of times, the intelligence officer made us file an incident report, with all the particulars. Just another paperwork shuffle. In the middle of September, we got the word the Airlift was going to cease on the last day of September 1949. Apparently, the Russians had had enough, and were going to open up the ground and water routes. Of course, they never could close the airplanes, but at least the pressure was not what it had been for the past 17 months.

The operations schedule had me flying in the afternoon of September 30. There was another 330th Squadron flight to fly just before General Cannon was to close the airlift, a great propaganda move. I called the tower, and said I had a problem with one of the engines, and the tower changed my takeoff so that I was taking off three minutes before Cannon. Just what the doctor ordered. Our aircraft was a C54G 435-566, with a load of 17,050 pounds of coal. It was a real thrill for me, for I could honestly say I flew the last full load of coal into Berlin. Cannon had only a token load, with mostly reporters.

Final approach to Rein-Main, to the southeast. May 1949.

Chapter Twelve
POST MORTEM

There were very few decisions that you could make while in the military. I can honestly say one of those times was when I volunteered to fly the Berlin Airlift. I loved flying, ever since my father, a World War I flier, took me up for a flight in a twin-wing World War I airplane, for a 30-minute flight out of the San Francisco Airport. It was a grass strip, but I didn't care. Since that time all I ever wanted to do was fly. After World War II I flew several airplanes, and it was quite an experience, but something was missing. My decision to fly on the Airlift was the best decision I ever made. It gives a pilot the confidence to fly anything, and under any conditions. It was gratifying to know that you could fly into any airport, under any weather conditions.

Those of us who did our job in Germany got some credit, that made us feel good, and we were trusted to fly the big boys around. I will never regret what happened in 1948 and 1949. After 30 years, including combat in Germany, Korea, and Vietnam, I knew what I was doing, and tried to help those who needed the confidence and stamina to do what was expected of them.

In 1951, the people of Berlin, in tribute to the fliers of the Berlin Airlift, erected a beautiful curved arch, in front of Templehof Aerodrome, to commemorate those fliers who had flown the "Luftbrucke," or Air Bridge. It still stands today, and is a living memorial to those who helped keep the Berliners alive during those critical days when the pilots and planes were the only ones who could bring the essentials of life to those who were cut off from the outside world.

The Congress of the United States, in 1951-52, authorized the award of the Medal of Humane Action, that was given to every pilot and flight engineer who participated in the Berlin Airlift. It is a cherished memento that has been cherished by those who participated. To my knowledge, that medal has not been awarded for any other action.